The Beauty of Running

Other books by Kim Chapin

BILLIE JEAN and TENNIS TO WIN
by Billie Jean King with Kim Chapin

Gayle Barron
with Kim Chapin

The Beauty
of Running

Harcourt Brace Jovanovich, New York and London

Requests for permission to make copies of any part of the work should be mailed to Permissions, Harcourt Brace Jovanovich, Inc. 757 Third Avenue, New York, N.Y. 10017

ILLUSTRATION CREDITS

Title p., pp. 19, 35, 41, 42, 48, 66, 68, 69, 70, 74, 75, 92, 110, 112, 145–65, 180, 187, 200, 201, 203, 213, 217: Jane Sobel and Arthur Klonsky/Janeart, Ltd.; pp. x–xi: Billy Grimes; pp. 11, 184: Norm Paschal; pp. 13, 14, 23: Ray Plante; p. 25: Peggy McMahon; p. 26: United Press International; p. 30: Bob Connell for Brown, Gray Ltd.; p. 45: Sarah Abram; pp. 50, 53, 54, 56, 58: Harcourt Brace Jovanovich Photo Studio; shoes courtesy of Brooks Manufacturing Company; pp. 61, 178: John E. Barrett; pp. 117, 131: Howard S. Friedman; p. 202: Horst Muller; p. 218: Flair Photographic.

Printed in the United States of America

HBJ

Library of Congress Cataloging in Publication Data

Barron, Gayle.
The beauty of running.

Bibliography: p.
Includes index.
1. Marathon running.   2. Running.
I. Chapin, Kim, joint author.   II. Title.
GV1065.B37   796.4′26   79-3343
ISBN 0-15-111401-3

Set in Linotype Times Roman

First edition

B C D E

In deepest love and memory to Mother and Daddy,
who will never have the opportunity to enjoy this book
but who were my biggest supporters
throughout my life,
in my running career and all the rest.

Acknowledgments

This book could not have been written without the knowledge and support of many people whose encouragement I am deeply grateful for.

To my husband, Ben, my eternal love and appreciation. Without his unwavering support and confidence, I would not have become the runner that I am. He has devoted many hours to make this book possible, giving the benefits of his own broad experience and insight into running.

Grateful thanks to Dr. Stan Dawson in Atlanta, whose beliefs in holistic health have helped change my life and who generously spent voluntary hours elucidating many concepts in this book for me and for the running public.

I would also like to thank Ben Vaughan, who helped on the chapter on injuries and who knows what it's like to experience pain.

I appreciate the help of my good friend Caroline Harkleroad, who worked hard to bring this book about.

Dr. Tim Singleton has coached me and gave me confidence during my early years as a runner, for which I am indebted to him.

The man who has been an inspiration to me ever since I met him in Boston in 1975, Dr. Ernst van Aaken, is responsible for the growth of women's long-distance running.

Jess and Julie Bell have become like a second family to me and have dedicated their lives to supporting running.

To my biggest fan, my brother Tommy, a special thank you.

And grateful thanks to all my running friends and acquaintances who have helped me train and believed in me, and who have made running the pleasure it is today for so many.

Contents

1 • Two Unforgettable Races
3

2 • Keeping Running in Perspective
31

3 • Outfitting Yourself
51

4 • Relaxing into Your Own Natural Style
67

5 • Trying Something New: Variety,
Speed Work, and Racing
93

6 • Stress and the Mind-Body System
113

7 • Running Pain and Injuries: Prevention
and Treatment
127

8 • A Whole Body Workout
141

9 • Energetic Eating
168

10 • Running and Beauty
179

11 • The Marathon Experience
185

12 • A Summing-Up
209

Suggestions for Further Reading
219

Index
221

The Beauty of Running

Two Unforgettable Races

Atlanta—December 16, 1972

The day began innocently enough. At nine-thirty in the morning, Ben, who is my husband, and I sat down to a leisurely Saturday breakfast in our northside Atlanta apartment. Ben, I suspect, sipped a milk shake with a couple of raw eggs mixed in because that's how he always starts the day. I no doubt nibbled at some poached eggs, with a slice or two of whole wheat toast, or maybe dabbled at a bowl of cold cereal.

The day promised to be totally unmemorable until Ben looked up with a grin on his face and said, "They're having a marathon over at Westminster [a nearby private school], and I'm gonna run in it. Starts at noon."

"Ben," I said after a very short pause, "you are *crazy*."

We had been married for three years and running for five. The farthest I had run was 8 miles, only once; the most Ben had done was 10 miles, I think twice. We did run regularly 4 to 5 miles a day—sixteen to twenty laps around the quarter-mile running track nearby at Northside High School about five or six times a week. I wasn't even sure what a marathon was, only that it involved doing things we had never done before, such as running in the streets and up and down hills, and that the distance—26 miles, 385 yards —was roughly five times as long as our average daily workout.

The whole project smacked of foolishness, to say nothing of sheer masochism.

"It's something I've wanted to try for a long time," Ben said. "Want to come along?"

He asked me, I later found out, hoping I would politely decline. He wasn't sure how well he could do on his own, and he certainly didn't want the responsibility of having to worry about someone else, even—especially—if that someone else was his wife.

I don't think I was a particularly competitive person back then. (Most of my running friends feel I'm still not.) There were few runners to compete against, and certainly no women. Whatever competitive instincts I had found their release in my daily workouts with Ben. But the idea that Ben might get in a solid 12 or 16 miles —or even the full 26—and jump ahead of me in our training must have bugged me a little. Maybe a lot.

I decided to give it a shot. "But," I added, "there's no way I can possibly do the whole thing."

"We won't run fast," said Ben. "We'll just see how much we can do."

Sure, I thought, as we prepared to leave. *Now we are both crazy.*

The race was the Peach Bowl Marathon, which was eight years old. By way of comparison, that year the Boston Marathon was run for the seventy-sixth time. Nowadays people run marathons for kicks and in great hordes—old people, young people, men, and women. But in 1972, running was not exactly the most popular pastime in the world, and marathoning was almost unheard of. Back then you were either serious about running a marathon and kept it to yourself, or you didn't run one.

Our ignorance was appalling. What did you wear to a marathon? We didn't know. I wore running shoes, but ones that were absolutely flat, without any cushioning whatsoever. The temperature was right around 55 degrees. That seemed fairly nippy, and I bundled up in a heavy sweat shirt. As we signed in at the Westminster gymnasium, we noticed people drinking water and fruit juices and Gatorade—anything liquid—but figured that could only make us sick. We didn't touch a drop. We saw several runners doing stretches and strides. Waste all that energy before a race? Nonsense.

Ben and I got a lot of raised eyebrows from our running friends, none of whom had any idea that we were in training for a marathon. Which, of course, we weren't. But no one tried to discourage or dissuade us, so we went ahead.

We learned that the course wound for 13 miles through the streets of northwest Atlanta, an area of beautiful, rolling hills, and that there were actually two races in one. Of the 200 or so entrants, two-thirds were signed up for the half marathon, consisting of one complete 13-mile circuit. The rest of us were in the marathon: twice around the course and a lap and a half of the Westminster running track at the finish.

Two women were entered. Gillian Valk wisely opted for the half marathon. In the full marathon, I had a lock on first place in the women's division. If I could finish.

Ben and I started out very slowly. In our training runs we usually did 5 miles in around 40 minutes—a pace of 8 minutes per mile—but now we just sort of shuffled around the first loop at about 10 minutes per mile. Really loafing. Ben, who is a very good pacer, led the way and kept turning around to ask how I felt. The answer was: surprisingly good. Having trained 4 to 5 miles per day, we found we could handle the first 13 miles without a whole lot of trouble, hills and all. We ran with a couple of guys, and the four of us just talked away and had a grand old time.

At the halfway point Ben again asked me how I felt, whether I wanted to stop.

"Frankly," I said, "I don't feel that awful. I don't know why, but I don't. Let's see if we can make it just a little bit farther."

Although we never said it out loud, I think we both got it into our heads right then that as long as we'd come that far, we might as well try to go the whole way. If the first 13 miles hadn't been so difficult, maybe the last 13 wouldn't be either. What did we know? Besides, once we passed the start-finish line and set out on the second loop, our options were limited. We could run the rest of the way, walk, or hitch a ride.

About a mile into the second loop there was this hill. It had been there the first time around, of course, but that was at the start of the race, and it hadn't been a problem. Now it became a very serious one. The hill was about three-quarters of a mile long, a steep grade that never seemed to end, and it just wiped us out. (It was little consolation when we found out later that the hill came close to wiping everybody out.) The pain was excruciating, in my legs, chest, arms—everywhere. We lost the two guys who'd run the first loop with us. They'd quit, and when people start quitting, it serves to remind you how bad you feel yourself.

Not that I needed reminding. There were tears in my eyes, and I remember thinking, *No way. There's no way I'm gonna finish this thing.*

I begged Ben to help me get up that hill. And he kept saying, "You can do it, Gayle. You can make it."

He kept encouraging me, although by that time he wasn't exactly feeling sprightly himself.

We made it up the hill, though I'm not sure how. We never walked, although we ran so slowly somebody watching us might have thought we did. At the top, the course flattened out. We picked up our pace again and felt a little better.

Then we came to Mount Paran Road. If it is springtime in Atlanta and you are in a car, Mount Paran Road is absolutely lovely. It runs over gentle, rolling hills and twists through woods that hide a succession of lavish homes. But if it is December, the woods are barren and bleak, and if you are running—or trying to run—those gentle, rolling hills seem to go on forever. It was a real bore, the second time around.

We were alone. It was just us and the cold, ragged sky and the folks at the aid stations. We had passed exactly one runner all afternoon, and the rest of the pack was long gone. A few friends out for a Saturday drive honked at us from their cars, but I doubt if they even knew what we were doing out there. Not many people ran marathons in those days, and even fewer watched them. It didn't seem like we'd ever get off Mount Paran.

Now we did start to walk, but then our legs tightened up, and pretty soon we couldn't even walk so well. Walking, in fact, was actually more painful than running, even though what we were doing at that point more nearly resembled a slow shuffle.

We were in trouble. We were very definitely in trouble. But Ben, ever the optimist, said, "We've gone this far. D'you think we can make it?"

What choice did we have? To me, it just seemed the sun was going down.

When we got to 20 miles, I thought, *Why quit now?* I'd never done 20 miles in my life. Six more weren't going to kill me. As we approached the finish, we even got a little pump of adrenaline, or something, and started running for real again. And I also realized —this must have been in my mind from the beginning, at least subconsciously—that if I did make it, I would be the first woman from the state of Georgia, and possibly the entire South, to have completed a marathon. *Everybody will be tremendously excited,* I told myself, *and it's all going to be very neat.*

Well, when Ben and I got back to Westminster for that last lap and a half around the running track, nobody was there except Billy Daniel, an official of the sponsoring Atlanta Track Club. He was holding the clock. He'd heard rumors that there were still three people out on the course somewhere: Ben and I and the fellow we'd both passed. (The last guy never did show up. I later found out he had picked up a ride and gone home.)

I was wiped out and very disappointed. All I wanted to do was cry.

Our time was 4 hours, 12 minutes.

Ben and I struggled on up to the gymnasium, where the awards were being handed out. They gave one to me, and I got a big round of applause. Everyone was fairly shocked that I'd even completed the race. I could hardly walk, I was so destroyed.

When I carefully eased myself back into my cold metal chair, the man sitting next to me asked, "You ever run a marathon before?"

"Nope," I said. "This is my first."

"How'd you train?" he asked.

"Train?"

"How far do you run each day?" he persisted.

"Oh, about four miles. Sometimes five."

"You're kidding!"

"No, I'm not."

"If you don't go home, right now, and soak in a hot tub for two hours, you are going to hurt for days."

Great. That painful realization was just dawning.

Then he told me I had just completed what was generally considered to be the hardest marathon course in the country.

That made me feel a little better. But not much.

Looking back, I realize that having run that first marathon, without any knowledge of distance running and without any real training, was probably the nerviest thing I'd done in my life. Also the stupidest. It was sort of like being the first person to climb Mount Everest—without a snow parka or an oxygen pack. And at the time there was very little about the race that I in any way considered daring or in which I took any pride.

Ben and I somehow made it home, and I took the long, soaking bath that had been recommended. I lay there for hours, with all the energy and high spirits of a limp and withered noodle. That night I could barely get to sleep. You know how achy you are when you've got the flu? How debilitating it is? This was three times worse.

The next morning I had to go to the bathroom, but I couldn't move. I couldn't even sit up. I had to roll myself gently out of bed and onto the floor and crawl to where I needed to go.

After two or three days the aches and pains and blisters began to go away, a little, and I started to feel better about the whole thing. But not much. I was honestly glad that I'd done it, but on balance I considered the whole affair mostly a horrible experience and was almost positive that I would never again run another marathon.

Boston—April 17, 1978

It is almost a paradox but nonetheless true that a world-class athlete in absolutely peak condition is also just one very short step away from total physical collapse. This holds for tennis players, weight lifters, baseball shortstops, and football defensive tackles—

you name it—and especially for distance runners. The trick is to walk the tightrope and not fall off. In the seven months leading up to the 1978 Boston Marathon I fought the good fight and eventually won it, but when that laurel wreath was placed on my head, and the medallion draped around my neck, I was the most surprised person in the state of Massachusetts.

In the fall of 1977 I ran three marathons in fourteen weeks— in Eugene, Oregon; New York City; and Honolulu—and that is a lot of marathoning. Probably too much. But I came out of them just fine and after a short rest resumed what for me was a fairly rigorous training schedule. I continued to average about 75 miles per week, building my training around one long run per week of approximately 16 miles and one good day of speed work. Some weeks my speed work consisted of intensive interval training, either on a flat track or up and down hills. Other weeks I found a 10,000-meter race somewhere and ran in that.

Then in late January I almost fell off the tightrope. I came down with the flu, the first time I'd been sick with anything since college except maybe the sniffles, and it knocked me for a loop. I was bedridden for a week and barely ambulatory for two more. For an entire month I did very little running at all. With Boston so close, I didn't see how I would be able to run the race seriously, and I felt there might even be no point in my making the trip at all. You get fairly intimate with your body after nearly twelve years of training. You learn to read it on a daily basis and also get to know what kind of shape it's going to be in two and three months down the road. I wasn't optimistic.

Besides, I wasn't even pointing for Boston, nor were most of the world's other top women marathoners. The race we were all most keen about was the Women's International, a marathon for women only that had first been held in 1974 in Waldniel, West Germany. The race's guiding force was—and is—a German doctor named Ernst van Aaken, who is one of the world's leading authorities on distance running and had conceived of the International as a way to persuade the West German sports federation, as well as that of other countries, that women could run distances up to and beyond the 26.2 miles of the marathon without dying or otherwise seriously harming themselves. In 1978 it was going to be

Dr. Ernst van Aaken has long been a vigorous crusader for women's distance running.

held in the United States for the first time. On March 19 in my hometown of Atlanta.

I resumed training in late February and for the next three weeks or so pushed through a lot of tiredness. The race itself was a killer, run over a course loaded with hills on a day that was exceedingly hot—78 degrees—and humid. I led for a while, carrying a sponge, which I used to squeeze great gobs of water over my head at every opportunity. (Ben, who was doing a radio commentary on the race, remarked that this was a sure sign of trouble—something about how my vanity wouldn't let me muss up my hair unless it was absolutely necessary.) Julie Brown of Northridge, California, one of America's top distance runners, broke from the pack to take the lead at about the 15-mile mark despite pleas from her coach, riding just ahead of her in a press van, to slow down. Six miles later she nearly collapsed and had to drop out. I faded and finished fifth, behind Marty Cooksey of Los Angeles, Manuela Angenvoorth of West Germany, Sarolta Monsport of Hungary, and Cindy Dalrymple of Honolulu; but under the circumstances I didn't feel my performance was all that shabby.

That left exactly four weeks to Boston. I continued to train with Ben and some of our friends, but I had to cut short nearly every one of my workouts. The three fall marathons, and then a month of the flu followed by a fourth long race, had taken their toll. Run Boston? No way.

In addition to a disconcerting lack of quality workouts, I had just celebrated my thirty-third birthday. While by distance-running standards that was not terribly ancient, it was pushing things a bit. Besides, I had never won a quality marathon. My personal record was 2 hours, 47 minutes, and I had accumulated a lot of seconds, thirds, and fourths, but except for a couple of races in Atlanta, where the competition was a handful of local women, I had never crossed the finish line ahead of the pack.

But . . . Ben was going, our friends were going, and I had skipped the 1977 race because of a pulled hamstring and didn't want to miss the spectacle two years in a row, and so I decided to go, too.

I knew people would expect a lot from me—not a win, but certainly a finish in the top ten and maybe even one in the top five—but what I really wanted to do was hang a sign around my neck that read: "I'm not really trying this time, folks."

I didn't even send in an entry. By the time I finally made up my mind the deadline had passed.

Boston was going to be a 26.2-mile fun run, and that's all.

Marty Cooksey and I before the start of the 1978 Avon Women's International Marathon, in Atlanta.

The Boston Marathon was first run in 1897, following by one year the modern revival of the Olympic Games. By tradition it is held on the third Monday in April to coincide with Patriot's Day, a holiday celebrated only in the Commonwealth of Massachusetts. Ben and I flew up several days early and checked into the Copley Plaza Hotel, where we shared a suite with Jess Bell, the president of the Bonne Bell cosmetics company, his son Buddy, and Steve Gladdis, a friend of ours from Cleveland. We didn't do much of anything, really, except absorb the Boston atmosphere and attend some of the clinics, exhibits, and receptions offered by the many equipment manufacturers and individuals with a stake in running, now that it had become big business. I wanted to write a magazine article on the race but couldn't find a publication that was interested. I had been doing some television work in Atlanta and thought it might be amusing to carry a small microphone and report on what it's like to run in the middle of the awesome Boston Marathon pack, but that fell through because the stations I contacted said it was too late to test the technical equipment. (The next year, 1979, I did carry a microphone and battery pack during the race for WBZ-TV, the NBC station in Boston, but it never got working right. All anybody could hear from me was a lot of static, and after 9 miles I detached myself from the thing and gave it to Ben, who gave it to a friendly policeman, who, I hope, gave it back to WBZ.)

I always cut back my mileage severely the last week before any marathon, but in the days leading to Boston my training was downright desultory. On Friday, three days before the race, a sore foot and a nagging ache in my leg convinced me just to hang around the Prudential Center, which served as the official race headquarters and was where the marathon would end. On Saturday, Ben and I did an easy 5 miles or so.

On Saturday night our friend Ray Plante gave a premarathon party. Ray, an ardent runner and photographer, introduced us to the incredible John Kelley, who has been running Boston for more than forty years. He won the marathon in 1935 and again in 1945. Now seventy-two years old, he continues to run it each year to the delight and amazement of the crowds who recognize and cheer him on.

Ben and I meet the legendary John Kelley
before the 1978 Boston Marathon.

On Sunday, I fully intended to get in a final warm-up run but never quite got around to it. I kept putting it off and putting it off, and pretty soon it was nearly dark. Ben and I jogged down to the Eliot Lounge, a favorite runners' hangout, and had some pizza and beer and jogged back. Total distance: one-half mile each way.

I almost forgot to pick up my official number, mainly because I didn't think there would be one for me. If I had to, I was quite prepared to run the race as an unofficial entrant, which is what a lot of people do anyway. But late Saturday afternoon Ben ambled down to the Prudential Center and found out that some friends had interceded on my behalf with Will Cloney, the delightful curmudgeon who, with Jock Semple, has been running the Boston Marathon forever, and with an iron fist. My number was 229, the last assigned to a woman.

The weather on Monday morning was perfect. The temperature was in the mid-40s, there was no wind, and a solid New England sky almost guaranteed at least a spittle of cooling rain. I was rested, relaxed, and pretty much unaffected by the excitement of the race.

The race was scheduled to begin precisely at noon. Starting at seven-thirty in the morning, shuttle buses provided by the sponsoring Boston Athletic Association began transporting a goodly portion of the 4,674 official entrants from the Prudential Center to the starting line in suburban Hopkinton, 26 miles to the west.

Ben and I declined the ride. A Boston friend of Jess Bell's picked us up at our hotel at nine-thirty and drove us out, and along the way we could already see a portion of what would be a mammoth crowd gathering at the choice locations along the course.

We went to the Hopkinton High School gymnasium, the traditional prerace gathering spot for the runners. (Also, it is the only place where you can change clothes.) It really isn't smart to spend the hour or two before a marathon just standing around, but in this case it was an opportunity to talk with old running friends I hadn't seen since the last time I'd run Boston and to begin to pick up the special air of the race.

The gym was a festival. There were runners from every state in the Union and a score of foreign countries, and for the vast majority of them just to have qualified for Boston was the highlight of their running careers. They were there to participate and to finish and perhaps to lower their personal time records, although

the huge number of starters would make the last nearly impossible for all but those in the first few rows. There was very little prerace gamesmanship or psyching going on, except perhaps among the top dozen or so men. There was a particular camaraderie among the best women runners. Most of us had known each other for at least a few years, and strong friendships had sprung up. If there was any psyching going on, it was a case of one woman's goading herself into the right frame of mind for the race and wasn't being done at the expense of anyone else. The running of a marathon—any marathon—is too personal a matter for that sort of thing to go on.

It is true, however, that no runner (and this applied to the men as well) was willing to admit that she was in great shape, felt super, and was raring to go. We all had our excuses. We hadn't trained enough or we had trained too much; we'd run too many long races recently or too few; our legs hurt or our feet hurt—and on and on. And looking around the gym at the other women, I felt that everybody *else* was skinny and healthy and ready to absolutely burn it.

Me? I was just out for a good time.

We moseyed over for the start. In previous years the race had begun on a little side street. You ran for about 50 yards to a sharp right-hand turn that led onto State Highway 135, and the jam-ups and general confusion were incredible. It was like pouring several thousand marbles down a chute that suddenly narrowed to a bottleneck, and it was absolutely essential to get a position near the front. In 1975, my first Boston, a running friend of Ben's and mine from Atlanta named Tim Singleton devised a strategy to keep several of us from getting lost in the pack. We sort of sneaked away from everybody on the pretext of having to go to the bathroom and walked over to a street parallel to the street where the starting line was. We did our stretches and strides and other warmups, and just a couple of minutes before noon we cut through some backyards and innocently trotted out in front of the starter. We got a few dirty looks, but we also saved ourselves from a lot of pushing and shoving.

In 1978 the starting line was moved directly onto Highway 135, and all the runners were seeded, by groups, according to their qualifying times. Along with several other women, I got a position

Ben and I prepare to challenge the awesome Boston pack.

in the first seeding. Ben was in the third group—not ideal, but still respectable. We took our positions, and that's the last I saw of him until the end of the race.

At noon the starter's gun sounded, and I ran for my life. There were several hundred faster men right behind me, we were all pumped up, and the first few hundred yards were slightly downhill. I knew I was going to get trampled, curve or no curve. I kept turning my head and shouting, "Don't run over me. I'll get out of your way."

I made a clean start. I caught a few elbows, and there was a lot of pushing and jostling for a while, but it wasn't nearly as bad as I thought it would be. But you know how you can hear when somebody falls next to you or behind you without really seeing him or her go down? I heard that dull thud three or four times. No

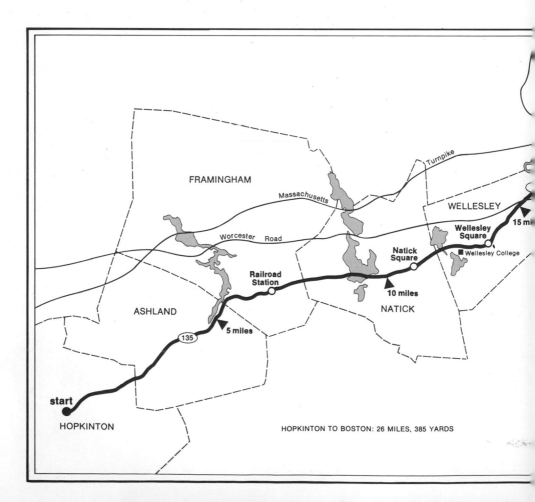

HOPKINTON TO BOSTON: 26 MILES, 385 YARDS

telling what happened to those people. (In 1979, when 7,877 of us started, it took more than 8 minutes for the last official entrants to reach the *starting* line.)

They say the first half of the course, from Hopkinton to Welles-ley, is slightly downhill. That's what *they* say, but I've never been able to sense that. To me, it's rolling flat. Still, nearly everybody runs hard. Your adrenaline is flowing, you're trying to establish your own rhythm, and the last thing you worry about is your pace or your place in the race.

And something else, too. No matter how good or bad you feel at the start, you never know how you're going to do in a marathon until you're well into the race. For both Ben and me, the first clues to what might happen to us came at the 5-mile mark. Ben, who was running slightly behind me—although he didn't know it—

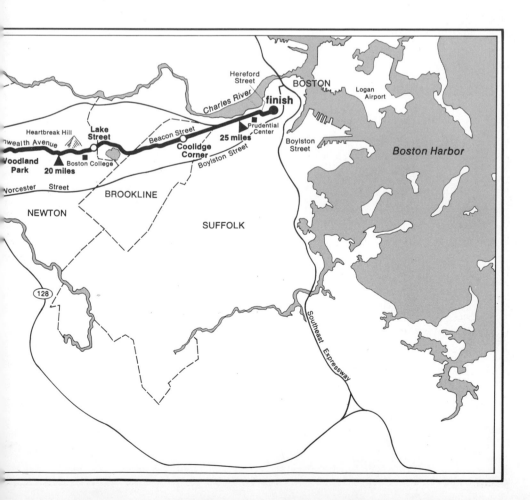

Settling in, with just 20 miles to go.

sensed that for him it was going to be a long afternoon. He'd had some problems with his left calf and was running on one wheel. Although he wasn't tired, he had no zip, no pep, and was already just going through the motions. When I got my 5-mile split, however, I knew I was going to be okay.

I didn't hear an official time called out, but a friend who had always run faster than I came up from behind and said we were on a 2-hour, 38-minute pace. I couldn't figure it out. I felt fine, but it scared me a little to know I was almost 10 minutes ahead of my best marathon time ever. I tried to stay relaxed. I concentrated on my footwork, my breathing, my arm swing—anything to help me keep the nice, easy rhythm I'd established. I wasn't worried about my placing among the women. It was too early for that, and anyhow, with just 229 of us scattered among the 4,445 men, it was impossible to tell with any certainty exactly who was where.

But 8 miles into the race—a mile on the far side of Framingham —I saw, or thought I saw, the bouncing pigtails of Kim Merritt about 50 yards in front of me.

Kim Merritt, of Racine, Wisconsin, was a great runner (and still is). In Eugene, Oregon, the previous September, she had set the American record of 2 hours, 37 minutes. No matter what kind of shape she was in, she always went out hard. Since I rarely did, I'd never been close to her in a race after the first couple of miles— never even *seen* her. Knowing that, I realized that either she was running very slowly or I was running very fast, probably too fast. I considered dropping back. Then I reconsidered and figured I'd hang in there as long as I could, even if it meant dropping out. That wasn't something I wanted to do, but it wasn't going to surprise anybody, least of all myself, if I did.

There was a reason for Kim's slow pace. The previous summer and fall she had entered a staggering total of sixteen races, ranging from 5-mile sprints to full marathons, in seventeen weeks and won them all. It was a tremendous accomplishment, but she had

Kim Merritt
hits her stride
at the 1979
Avon Women's
International
Marathon.

run herself into the ground and was now paying the price. It didn't help that she had won Boston in 1975 and had finished second in 1977. The pressure of being expected to repeat a good performance only added to her burdens.

I got closer and closer and finally caught up with her just outside Natick. Kim was running with her husband, Keith, who often paced her, and they both did a double-take. They weren't used to seeing me any more than I was used to seeing them.

I usually don't like to run arm and arm with another woman, especially if we're racing for a high finishing position. It's too easy to get sucked into a pace that's not your own, which in a marathon can be fatal, and frankly, I hadn't had much experience at it. I had run just two women-only marathons, the Internationals at Waldniel in 1976 and in Atlanta the month before. It was a strange feeling to be running with the competition.

The three of us—Kim, Keith, and I—ran together for the next several miles. Kim and I talked some, encouraging each other and wondering out loud about rumors that at least one other woman was up the road ahead of us. Another runner said yes, the woman from Fort Lauderdale was about a quarter-mile in front, and we knew that would have to be Gayle Olinek. We assumed Gayle was leading, but we really didn't know, and there was no way to find out.

Wellesley College, the women's school, marked the halfway point, and naturally all the women runners received tremendous cheers. For Kim and me the applause was deafening. Not only were we women, but we were running neck and neck, probably for second place. Even though there were 13 miles to go, the spectators could sense a real race developing.

Keith backed off after we passed through Wellesley, leaving Kim and me to run alone. We didn't say too much after that. The crowds began pressing close, leaving only a narrow funnel for us to run through, and it was time to start thinking about Heartbreak Hill. Things were getting serious.

We passed Gayle Olinek right before the start of Heartbreak Hill. She had gone out too fast and was falling back. I couldn't be 100 percent sure, but I was almost certain that Kim and I were now running for first place. Amazing. I was undertrained, I had gone out too fast, I was running shoulder to shoulder with Amer-

I felt strong and comfortable throughout the 1978 Boston run.

ica's top distance runner—and yet I felt strong. I felt so good, in fact, that I knew it couldn't last. Something had to go wrong.

Heartbreak Hill is actually four rises, each one steeper and longer than the one before it—at least it seems that way—connected by three stretches that are almost perfectly level. There are no downhill sections, and when you reach the last crest, you are just 5 miles away from the finish line. Because Heartbreak Hill comes so late in the race, it is the most critical part of the Boston Marathon. I knew that if I did it well, the rest of the race would be a breeze; if I did it badly, there would be no time left to make amends.

Kim and I took turns leading over the entire 4 miles. She is a very good hill runner, and when she jumped ahead by 25 yards going up the first rise, I thought, *This is it. This is where she leaves me.* But on the first flat I caught up to her again. We ran dead even up the second and third rises, the crowds screaming in our ears. As we started up the fourth rise, Kim began to fall back, but I figured she would catch up again when we reached the last crest. She looked strong, and I felt comfortable, and I really thought that's the way we'd stay—glued together—right until the end.

But it didn't happen that way. Kim stayed close for another mile or so after the hill, to where the course jogs from Commonwealth Avenue onto Beacon Street, but then I began to stretch my lead. Just like that. We didn't say anything or otherwise acknowledge what was happening. It just happened.

I know this will sound corny, but a part of me didn't want to pass Kim. We had become pretty close during the previous year, and I wanted her to be able to run strongly right to the finish line. If Kim had been somebody I didn't particularly care for, I wouldn't have felt that way, but I knew how much pressure she was under and how much more important the race was to her than to me.

But I also realized I couldn't worry about that sort of thing, no matter what, and kept building my lead.

Ben was 5 minutes behind me—less than a mile—and although I didn't know it, he was seeing the race from an unusual perspective. First, he caught up with Keith Merritt, who told him that Kim and I were probably running for second place. He was shocked. Then he passed Gayle Olinek and ran for a while with Lauri Pedrinan, another top runner. By then he knew—better than I, almost—that unless there was some mystery woman nobody was aware of, Kim and I were no longer fighting for second but for the whole ball of wax. Keeping track of the women was a nice diversion for him. It helped him forget how he felt, which was pretty awful. He just wanted the race to be over with.

I felt fine. I was dressed out in a well-worn pair of Brooks Vantage training shoes. Normally I would have worn a pair of lighter racing shoes, but I had pulled my right hamstring the year before and the Brooks Vantages were the only shoes I owned that eased the dull and persistent ache in the back of my leg. In fact, the only pain I felt wasn't a pain at all: the big toe on my right foot was numb.

There I was, leading the most famous marathon in the world and thinking, *Geez, I wish I could feel my big toe.*

As I said, if you can get past the hills in good shape, the rest of the course is pretty easy. But when I think back, I realize that the women closest to me weren't all that far away. If I had faltered just a little, or if I had eased up, somebody could have caught me.

Near the finish the crowd urged me on, but made passing difficult.

But by then I felt so positive about what was happening that I really didn't think anybody would.

Down Beacon Street and through Coolidge Corner I was pulled along by the crowd, almost literally. The police estimated that more than 800,000 people lined the course. Crowd control everywhere was something of a joke, especially over the last 4 miles. The spectators yelled and screamed so loudly that I wanted to put my hands to my ears. That part I loved, but near the end the crowd pressed so close to the runners that we literally had to run single file. We couldn't weave in and out of a pack, and my technique for passing people was to tap them on the shoulder, say, "Excuse me," and hope they moved out of the way. The other runners were all very good about that—they'd jump aside and give a word of encouragement—but everybody could have knocked a couple of minutes off his or her time if the course had been wider.

Crowds also lie. Unintentionally, of course, but they still feed you false information. They'll shout, "One mile to go," and then you run a mile, only to discover there's still another mile left. If you don't know the course, that can be devastating.

While all this was going on, I was also still trying to find out who was leading the race. I was fairly certain I was, but I didn't know for sure, and neither did anyone else. I was surrounded by hundreds of men, and I couldn't be absolutely certain that some-body—the crowd, the other runners, or I—hadn't missed a woman in front of me.

Two men started pacing me. They weren't people I knew, just friendly runners who told me I looked strong and reminded me to stay relaxed. Then a couple of other guys came up and said there was a woman in pigtails just a few minutes behind me. This was one of those good news/bad news deals. The good news was that both Kim Merritt and Gayle Olinek wore pigtails, and neither one had looked particularly strong the last time I'd seen her. The bad news was that a lot of women wear pigtails, including one that might have been sprinting to the finish. (The woman in pigtails turned out to be Penny DeMoss of Los Altos, California, who finished second.)

Right at Coolidge Corner, with less than a mile and a half to go, I panicked. I started running harder and harder. Until that moment I hadn't thought a lot about winning the race, just about lowering my personal record and maybe, with luck, finishing in the top two or three. But then I started wondering what I would do— what I could do—if somebody passed me. Would I have enough left to pass her before the end?

I reached the last zigzag. I turned right and ran uphill for a quarter of a mile to the Prudential Center and turned left—and saw the finish line just 100 yards away. It was a beautiful sight, and I sprinted as hard as I could.

I *still* didn't know whether I'd won. People were shouting that I had, but I still didn't know—until two policemen grabbed me by the arms. I remembered pictures of Kim crossing the finish line in 1975, and that Boston's finest were there to greet you first.

Boston's finest greet me at the finish line.

I was just wantin' to be up there forever.

"Did I win?" I shouted. "Did I win?" I was grinning foolishly, relieved and happy at the same time.

The policemen assured me that I had. They pushed their way through the crowds, with me in tow, to a platform in front of the Prudential Center, where the wife of Boston's mayor put a laurel wreath on my head and draped a medal around my neck. It was the peak experience of my life—it was like it must be at the Olympic Games when you win a gold medal and stand at attention while the national anthem is played. I didn't want to leave.

In a few minutes somebody said, "It's time to get down, ma'am."

But I was just wantin' to be up there forever.

To understand our victory party that night, you have to know a little about Jess Bell. He had turned fifty-three earlier that year, looked forty, and was in excellent shape. For reasons I'll explain later, he was, and is, one of distance running's greatest ambassadors, and of course, he is a marathoner. Despite being the president of a fairly large and very successful cosmetics company, he is very likely to walk into a fancy restaurant wearing a sports coat and a T-shirt with something like "Go Tiger" written across the front. Which, along with a cowboy hat and a pair of running shoes, is precisely what he had on when several of us trooped into a private dining room at Locke-Ober, one of those proper Bostonian restaurants with a lot of dark wood that looks like it dates from the Revolution and probably does. (Locke-Ober used to be a private club, I understand, and, until not too many years ago, refused to admit women. A nice irony that night.)

The dinner was not planned as a victory party. Nobody had the foggiest notion I was going to win the race. Jess had simply arranged a quiet evening for Ben and me, his son, and a couple of other folks from his company just to celebrate all of us having run Boston. Period. But then, after things worked out the way they did, he was kind enough to invite several Atlanta runners who had trained with Ben and me, and along with spouses and friends, the number of people in our party had grown to almost twenty.

It was a marvelous evening. I had won, clocking in at 2:44:52. We had all set personal records—except Ben, who had run hurt— and everybody was in high spirits long before the spirits arrived. The food was superb, the beer and wine flowed freely, and by the end of the evening we were all about three sheets to the wind. Absolutely looped. (We really didn't have that much to drink, but it doesn't take a whole lot to set you on your ear after you've run a marathon.) And somehow the room suddenly became festooned with streamers of toilet paper—a throwback to college days—and I couldn't have felt better.

Then the check arrived. We all broke out in giggles. The entrées had been only around $8.95 on up, I think, but the tab was in the vicinity of $600. The only thing we could figure was that sometime during the festivities a waiter must have suggested more wine and Jess, ever the perfect celebrant, must have said, "Bring me your best."

Wish I could tell you what it was.

Jess gamely pulled out a credit card, smiled, and said, "Good luck."

The waiter smiled right back, a little stiffly, I thought, and spent

an inordinate amount of time clearing things before he let us go—
no doubt checking whether this guy in the T-shirt and cowboy hat
was really who his plastic said he was.

Ben and I went back to our hotel and got into bed. Ben closed
his eyes and dozed off. I tried but couldn't.

Two hours later, when it was obvious I was still so keyed up I'd
never get any rest, I tapped him on the shoulder.

"You asleep?" I asked.

"I was until now," he mumbled.

We talked about the race some more, and I wished the night
would never have to end.

In the months both preceding and following the marathon, two
very significant personal events took place in my life. To tell of
them here may seem out of place, but both had a very real and
direct relationship to what happened in Boston. Three months
before the race, I accepted Christ; two months after it, I lost
my father.

It was a small miracle that I was even able to go to Boston. At
best, I should have been laid up in an Atlanta hospital. At worst,
I should have been dead.

One afternoon the preceding August I was driving my car down
a long, steep hill not far from our apartment. It was raining hard,
a torrential southern summer rain, and I suddenly began to hydro-
plane wildly out of control. I slammed into a telephone pole and
destroyed the front end of my car. I wasn't wearing a seat belt, and
on instinct—there wasn't much time to think about it—I jumped
into the passenger seat an instant before a second car hit mine
broadside in the driver's door. A third car then smashed into the
first two. Nobody was hurt or even scratched, and I didn't think
too much about it right away. But I became convinced somebody
up there had protected me.

Two days later, for no obvious reason that I could discern, a
friend invited me to a Bible study class at her church. It is hard to
explain what happened over the next several months, but the
pieces seemed to fit, and I found myself willing to accept Christ
as my Savior. And in January I did.

I think that one reason I was able to accept Christ so easily was
because of my father. In his youth and early adulthood, he had

been a healthy, energetic, athletic man. Then, in the late 1950s, he contracted multiple sclerosis. He went from a cane to a pair of crutches to a wheelchair and finally, in 1970, to his bed. He knew, of course, that the disease was progressive and irreversible, and it was terrible for all of his family—my mother, my brother, and me —to watch him suffer. But he carried on with an inspirational inner strength and was at peace.

I ran the Boston race for my father. I had plenty of time to think during this marathon, not just about whether Kim Merritt or Gayle Olinek was gaining on me at the end or why my big toe was numb. I thought about my father a great deal, and I prayed. A tremendous amount of strength was given to me that day.

After I got my laurel wreath and medal and talked with the press, Ben and I walked back to our hotel and called his family, and then mine. Everybody was ecstatic, especially my father. He sounded even happier than I was.

Mother said, "I'm glad you won this year," and I think we both knew what she meant.

My father died two months later.

The night he passed away, I had a dream in which there appeared a letter from my father. In it, he said that he was very tired, but that he was going to a place where he wanted to be. He asked me to take care of my mother and to keep up the good work.

My victory at Boston . . . my Christian witness . . . my father's death. I think there was a connection. There had to be.

Keeping Running
in Perspective

The last time I heard, there were somewhere in the vicinity of 25 million runners of various sizes and descriptions scurrying about the highways and byways of America, and no doubt countless millions in other parts of the world as well. Jimmy Carter jogs his 3 miles a day on the White House lawn, and Paul Newman gets in his run whether he's on location or about to strap himself into one of those sporty race cars he sometimes drives on the weekends. So do Phyllis George, Bess Myerson, and Kate Jackson, and they are joined, at least in spirit, by my gynecologist, dentist, chiropractor, and, occasionally, the fellow who's helping me write this book (though his dedication is often suspect).

The running boom is still going strong despite a common hunch that it was only a fad. I can't really explain how or why it happened, but I have some ideas. In 1968 a doctor by the name of Kenneth Cooper published a book called *Aerobics*. Two years later he published a second one, *The New Aerobics*. Together they showed in a very programmatic way how average out-of-shape people could whip themselves into reasonably good physical condition in a minimum of time—an attractive idea to folks who operated on tight schedules. Running was the key.

Then, in 1972, Frank Shorter won the Olympic marathon in Munich, proving that Americans could run long distances just as well as the Africans and Europeans who had for so long domi-

Ben and I run together whenever and wherever we can.

nated that prestigious event. Finally, in the summer of 1977 Farrah Fawcett-Majors appeared full-blown on the cover of the trendy gossip magazine *People*, jogging with her then husband, Lee. That made running both glamorous and fashionable, and that's just about all it needed to gain widespread and popular acceptance. (Don't laugh. The skiing boom of the 1960s was partly attributed to the invention of stretch pants, and the tennis explosion of the early 1970s to the marketing of clothes in colors other than traditional country-club white. Things often become popular for mysterious reasons, but sex appeal and fashion never hurt.)

Nor is there any sign that the boom has peaked. The 1979 Boston Marathon attracted those 7,877 official entrants despite stringent qualifying standards—3 hours for men and 3 hours, 30 minutes for women and men over forty—and marathoning is only the tip of the running iceberg. In my hometown of Atlanta, the Peachtree Road Race, a traditional 10,000-meter run held on the Fourth of July, draws more than 20,000 entries—the winner crosses the finish line not very long after the last starter hits the starting line. No doubt your local paper lists a plethora of events you could enter almost every weekend, from 1- and 2-mile fun runs on up. I travel a lot, and I know I could run three quality races a weekend, if I chose and if my body let me. Which it won't. And with 1980 being an Olympic year, I'm sure that the most casual sports fan will be inundated with even more news from the distance-running front.

Helping report on and promote the running boom has been a predictable explosion in running literature. We are bombarded by newspaper columns, magazine articles, and a staggering number of books, all with their own graphs, charts, timetables, theories, and hunches, that presume to tell us how to run, what happens to us when we run, and what to wear while we run.

Why then another book, when too much has been made of running already?

To look at running in a very different way.

I'm surprised it took so long for running to catch on. But then again, I'm not. For decades the image of a distance runner was that of a guy—few women ran back then—with hollow cheeks and spindly legs who ran with a perpetual stitch in his side and blisters the size of silver dollars on his feet and breasted the tape at the end of his race one heartbeat this side of his Final Reward. The first distance runner of note, remember, was Pheidippides, the Greek who ran from the plain of Marathon to the streets of Athens with the news of a great victory over the Persians, then died. (Revisionist historians now wonder if his name wasn't really Philippides and why he didn't take a horse if his message was so important.)

One of the most compelling film clips in all sports shows English runner Jim Peters entering Vancouver (B.C.) Stadium near the end of the marathon in the 1954 British Empire Games. Peters, a former world record holder in the event, is several minutes ahead of the field. He needs only to jog one lap around the running track—he could have walked—to win the laurel wreath. But he has hit the wall, solidly and smashingly. He is exhausted, feeble, and disoriented, and he begins to stagger the wrong way. Then he collapses, repeatedly and pathetically, and never does complete his race.

That one incident probably set back distance running for the masses by at least ten years.

Running also used to be associated with punishment, especially in athletics: "You missed that tackle, boy. Let's see some laps." And in the military: "Lift those knees, private. Let's hear some *enthusiasm*."

Even literature got into the act. In 1960 British author Alan Sillitoe wrote a novel called *The Loneliness of the Long-Distance Runner*. Of course, Sillitoe's book was about a lot more than running, but the title alone was enough to reinforce the connection between pain and even the most casual jogging. Running might be healthy (though that was still a matter of some debate), but if it was so terribly lonely, it certainly couldn't be much fun. Books on running were themselves often intimidating. One in particular was called, chillingly, *Be Fit! Or Be Damned!*

When running did emerge from the closet, thanks to Cooper, Shorter, Farrah Fawcett, and Lord knows who and what else, it came out blaring and blazing. Almost overnight it went from being an activity pursued by only a small band of dedicated aficionados to becoming perhaps the most popular form of recreation in this country. Unfortunately, but I suppose inevitably, a few folks got carried away and tried to give running an importance it simply didn't have. These proselytizers told us that running was different, that not only did it expand the lungs and pep up the heart, but it also transported the runner into a state of euphoric bliss so mystical that it could be understood only by other runners. These true believers proclaimed that the very act of running somehow placed the runner a cut above the rest of society—or at the very least outside its boundaries—where he or she was free to operate under a different set of rules from the rest of us.

The backlash was not long in coming. In 1978 the city manager of Los Altos Hills, California, proposed a ban on running along public roads entirely. He claimed joggers packed up five and six abreast and refused to yield to traffic. Two out-of-shape sportswriters from New York City, Vic Ziegel and Lewis Grossberger, poked fun at the mystique of running in a slim best-seller called *The Non-Runners' Book*. It was dedicated to Calvin Coolidge, who said, "I do not choose to run." *Time* magazine chided the self-importance of what it labeled the True Runner. "Nothing vindicates any image of runners as . . . the most exemplary form of human beings ever," intoned *Time*'s essayist. "At the rate they are going they may win, by more than a nose, the crown as smuggest. . . . Granted their direction, the theologians of this ancient activity are well on their way to running running right into the ground."

That hasn't happened yet, nor is it likely to. But while running is not the lonely, agonizing pursuit it was once thought to be, neither is it a panacea for the ills of mankind, as some of today's philosopher-runners would have us believe. As far as I have been able to determine, there is absolutely nothing mysterious about running, and done knowledgeably and sensibly, it involves very little pain. Running is healthy, fun, and simple. Everything else you need to know about it follows from those three facts, and that is what this book is all about.

Anybody can run. If you can walk to the water cooler, as the saying goes, you can jog to the corner. And if you can jog to the corner, the quantity and quality of your running will be limited only by your genes, your inclination, and the amount of time you choose to spend at it.

My husband, Ben, and I give several clinics each year, and at most of them we show a film. One of the stars is a woman you

Anybody can run.

have never heard of named Eula Weaver. Eula runs regularly these days and has even entered a race or two, but at one time she was a bedridden invalid, suffering from most of the traditional infirmities of old age. Her doctor gave it to her straight. "Eula," he said, "you can either lie there and let them feed you with a spoon, or you can get out of your bed and start walking."

Eula thought about that for a while and said, "I'm going out on the roads tomorrow."

That was in 1973, when Eula was seventy-two.

Just the other day a newspaper here in Atlanta told the story of a man named Thomas Pagan, who lives in Pompano Beach, Florida. Pagan had been bouncing in and out of hospitals for years with a series of heart, lung, and blood diseases, and in mid-1977 his doctor gave him six months to live. Pagan was determined to beat the odds or, as he put it, commit suicide trying. He threw away his medication and, although he had never before done anything athletic, started walking. One thing led to another, and in January 1979, Pagan ran a marathon. His time of 6 hours, 33 minutes would hardly be a threat at Boston, but it did set a United States record—for eighty-year-olds.

Those are extreme examples, to be sure, but the running world is laced with them. The story of my good friend Jess Bell is instructive.

Several years ago Jess was viewing the world through the bottom of a martini glass, and his life was in shambles. (I'm not revealing any confidences here. Jess tells this story on himself whenever he gets the chance.) His marriage was going down the drain, and he had lost all interest in his business. Finally, his wife, Julie, left him, a jolt that caused Jess to take stock of himself. He swore off whiskey for 100 days. After a few weeks he found he felt better and was waking up earlier. To fill this new time on his hands, he took up running. Thirty days later he called Julie and asked her to come back. She did. Now both are accomplished marathoners and among running's most visible and vocal ambassadors. Every now and again, in fact, Jess throws open his sports coat to reveal a T-shirt (he has quite a collection) that reads: "Start Running Around with Your Wife."

A couple of years ago race-car driver Darrell Waltrip became so incensed by the sloppy work being done by the members of his pit crew that he made daily running a condition of their employment. Perhaps it was coincidence, but over the next several months his team developed into one of the most tightly knit operations in racing, and Waltrip himself emerged as a full-fledged star on the Grand National circuit, the most prestigious in stock car racing.

Most people, however, take up running for reasons less dramatic than a doctor's warning of impending death, the threatened breakup of their marriage, or an ultimatum from the boss. Running is such an individual and personal sport that there are probably as many reasons why people run as there are people running. Ben and I now run simply because we enjoy the anticipation of our daily workouts, feel good during them and even better after we're through. And I suspect that if you cut through the strange and often obtuse

Jess and Julie Bell, dear friends and two of my favorite runners.

language runners use among themselves, their motives would be similarly uncluttered.

But in the beginning it was different. Ben is one of those people who easily puts on weight. When he was a teenager, he stopped growing taller one summer but continued to grow wider. It took him a year and a half of constant exercise, mainly running and working out with weights, to get trim again. For two years after that, his motivation for running was the fear that if he didn't, he would quickly regain the excess weight that had proved so difficult to lose. Now Ben's hooked, and running is as natural for him as brushing his teeth. Although he still enjoys marathon racing and is constantly looking to lower his personal record, he would continue to run even if it were impossible for him ever again to enter formal competitions, at any distance.

As for me, I took up running in 1966, when I was an undergraduate at the University of Georgia, because I wanted to be with Ben.

So. Why should *you* run? I wouldn't presume to answer that question unless I could meet you personally and learn something of your medical history and a little bit about your psychological makeup as well. But I have gotten to know several hundred runners over the years, at least casually, and I've found that their reasons both for starting to run and for sticking with it fall into several rather broad categories. Perhaps one or more of them will ring a bell with you.

Running clears the head. Running is mindless, in the best sense of that word. The mechanics of running are so natural that they are easily learned by beginners and soon become automatic and instinctive, something that can't be said for the fundamentals of most other sports. Thus, while your body gets a workout, your mind is left free to cleanse itself of the many problems with which it must constantly deal, to reconsider old ideas and receive new ones, or simply to daydream.

One company president I know gladly extends his employees' lunch hour by 30 minutes, with the stipulation that they use the extra time to run or exercise in other ways. He realizes that the solutions to complicated problems often reveal themselves when our minds are uncluttered and that fresh ideas sometimes sneak in the side door of our brain when we're not really looking for them. (As an unanticipated bonus, this particular company also received substantial refunds on its medical insurance premiums.) Harry Truman took his famous daily walks as much to organize his thoughts as he did to exercise his body, and novelist Franz Kafka got much of his dark inspiration while pounding the streets of Prague.

One acquaintance of mine composes speeches while he runs; another carries a notebook to jot down the ideas that pop into his head. I don't, but I often wish I did. I come up with some absolutely brilliant thoughts while I'm running—and forget them completely by the time I get home.

Running relieves mental stress. Probably the largest single category of runners is composed of those for whom daily workouts offer a temporary respite from the tensions of their everyday lives. Think about it. We live in a very competitive society—in my opinion, too competitive. Too often we are like players on a foreign stage, where our performances are measured against standards not of our own choosing. This happens not only at work, where we have quotas to fill or deadlines to meet, but in our personal and social lives as well. I'm sure you've had days when you've tried like the dickens to get things done but just haven't been able to accomplish anything. I know I have. Maybe you didn't quite get the house cleaned or pay all the bills, or perhaps the business deal didn't work out the way you might have liked.

Whatever. It's on days like this I'm most thankful for my running because running is just about the least competitive form of recreation there is—or it should be—and hence one of the least mentally stressful. There is nobody out there telling you what to do or how fast to do it. You can set your own goals, then modify them according to your mood and how you feel, and that's it. When I finish, I feel relaxed, and if I were a car, I would think I'd just had my battery recharged. I have accomplished *something* on this otherwise frustrating day. Besides, it beats two aspirin or a double martini.

Running gives you time to yourself. Just as running offers a release from the demands of your work and your personal and social lives, so it is a pleasant escape from the people who make those demands. If you do everything you think you need to do during a day, and do it well, you can easily wind up with absolutely no time to yourself. Now, I'm not opposed to altruism—far from it—but I also don't believe there's anything wrong with being a little bit selfish and setting aside 20 or 30 minutes a day, even more, just for yourself alone. And if you regularly use that time for running, in a few months you will have built something of your own that's as solid and as tangible as a brick wall.

Running is a great confidence builder, especially for women. I couldn't have said that when I started running. In 1966 there were so few women running—so few runners, period—that we all had to be fairly self-confident or we never would have taken up the sport in the first place. But during the past four or five years, as the women's liberation movement and the fight for the ratification of the Equal Rights Amendment have become a part of our everyday lives, I have found that more and more women use running as a way to assert their independence, and I think it's great.

I must have heard the same story a hundred times. The woman is anywhere between thirty and fifty years old. When she was a child, all the athletic equipment under the Christmas tree was for her brothers. Her only try at sports came in her high school gym class, where she did some calisthenics and learned the rules for volleyball and field hockey, and she tolerated all this only because it was mandatory, two or three hours per week. Then she got married and had children, and since then she has spent most of her life subservient to the demands of her husband's career and the obligations of raising a family. Her husband plays golf or tennis and occasionally invites her along, but she doesn't have the background to learn these games well enough to enjoy them, and so she gives them up. Then along comes running. No particular skills required for that, and she gives it a shot.

Amazing. Her progress is steady, and the results are concrete. Perhaps she loses a few pounds or at least redistributes them. She feels better. She runs faster, and she runs longer. She is actually doing something on her own, and doing it rather well. This gives her confidence, improves her self-esteem—and her relationship with her husband changes, for the better, as it does with her kids and her friends. All because she's found an activity that is hers and hers alone.

I know that this might sound farfetched and that I'm beginning to proselytize a little myself, but check around among your running friends and see if I'm not right. It happens all the time.

Running can be overdone, of course, just like anything else. At one clinic Ben and I hosted at Hilton Head, South Carolina, one of the day's programs began with a moderate run of 30 to 45 minutes. When we reassembled, one of the women in our group was missing. She didn't show up for another 2 hours.

Later in the day her husband cornered Ben and me, and he was absolutely distraught. It turned out that she did this frequently —just took off jogging down the road for 2 and 3 hours at a time. He wanted to run with her, but she didn't want to run with him, and for him, at least, running was becoming a totally negative experience.

Obviously there were underlying problems in their relationship. He was a lawyer who worked long hours seven days a week, and his wife was using running to escape from a life-style that didn't exactly thrill her.

Sue and Pete Petersen, husband-and-wife marathoners
who often race together.

Running couples share the good times.

In their case, running was a symptom of a bad marriage rather than the cause of it.

It's fine for a woman to use running as a means to achieve independence, but not at the expense of her marriage and family.

Whenever possible, I encourage husbands and wives, and even entire families (or just good friends), to run together. This doesn't conflict with what I said earlier about running's being an individual activity. It is, but it's obvious—to me, anyway—that sharing something with your mate, or someone else you care about, is more enjoyable than going it alone. And the obvious fact that two people aren't necessarily going to run at the same pace doesn't have to be a problem either. Often the man is faster than the woman, or is capable of running longer and farther, but you'll be surprised how easy it is for two people, with a little judicious pacing and encouragement on the part of the more experienced runner, to enjoy running together even if they are at different levels. The main idea is to be out there together.

Several years ago at the Women's International Marathon in Waldniel, West Germany, I saw the results of a survey of top women marathoners, including myself. The study showed that most of the women who were divorced or having problems with their mates were aggressive and independent. Nothing surprising there. What was surprising was how radically my answers differed from most of the others', mainly because I was happy with my home life. (The questions were along the lines "Do you enjoy cooking for your husband?" and things like that.) Still, I was told by more than one world-class runner that if I continued to run and do well at it, there was no way my marriage could last, that eventually my husband wouldn't be able to handle the publicity, the praise, and the constant travel. Nonsense.

At every level of running, though, there is the danger that if you aren't careful, you can become consumed by it. This applies as much to men as to women. I am totally frustrated by today's society. Everybody overdoes everything, including running. Running ought to be simple, relaxing, and fun, and entirely too many people try to turn it into work. They insist on being competitive with their friends, their neighbors, and their own stopwatches, and they are distraught and dismayed if they don't see measurable improvement every time they hit the pavement.

This syndrome shows up everywhere. A woman enters an annual 10,000-meter race in her hometown. The first year she has a great time running in the middle of the pack or maybe even near the end of it. She's satisfied with having completed the 6.2-mile run regardless of her time, and she feels great. Then she thinks, *Aha. Next year I'm gonna better my time, and I'm gonna train like the dickens so I can.*

So the next year she shows up again; only this time one look at her eyes tells you she's itchy, irritable, hyperactive, and wound tighter than a spring. For her, running has stopped being fun and has become work. Running no longer helps her release her tensions; it adds to them. Which defeats the whole purpose.

I see that sort of thing every year in Atlanta. Thousands of people begin training for the July 4 Peachtree Road Race sometime in February or March. They really work hard, trying to get themselves into super shape for that one big event of the year. Then they get hurt and have to miss the race. Or on race day it's so hot —not unusual down here—that they run a bad race. They are distraught, and they pack away their running gear until the following spring, when they go through the whole drill once again.

But if you consider running as a lifetime activity, one you're going to stick with despite the inevitable ups and downs, a minor injury or one bad race can't possibly bother you. It apparently takes some doing for certain kinds of people to get into this frame of mind, but believe me, they're better off when they do.

Then there are the streakers, who in my opinion are even more obsessed and self-defeating. Streakers, in jogging jargon, are runners who cannot bear to miss a day on the road. I know one poor fellow up in north Georgia who has trained every day for the past ten years, though his running hasn't improved for the last eight. Other runaholics make New Year's resolutions never to miss more than three or four days a year. I never think that way. It puts you under too much stress right from the start. It's like when you were in college and the course instructor gave you four free cuts at the beginning of the semester. When on earth do you take them? If you feel like sleeping in, do you play hooky, or do you save those precious off days for when you really need them? Decisions like that used to drive me crazy.

People who think this way feel they're somehow going to lose ground if they miss a day or two. That's just plain silly. You can't possibly lose that much by missing a day, and in fact, an occasional day off from your schedule, no matter what its intensity, will probably help your running more than it will hurt it.

There is another kind of overachiever. These are the mileage nuts. They can tell you to the fraction of a mile how far they ran yesterday, last week, last month, and last year. I couldn't. If you asked me how many miles I ran in January 1980, I'd have to look it up in my little black book.

Yes, I do keep track of my mileage, but only for informational purposes. I run according to how I feel on a given day, then jot down the mileage or the time. It's helpful to be able to check how much I ran before a certain race, or how hard I was training just before I pulled a certain muscle, because information like that can help me rough out my training program in the future. But I don't adhere to a rigid, inflexible schedule, and you don't have to either, as I'll show you. It's just not necessary.

A quick word about kids. Every now and again you read about preteenagers who are doing awesome amounts of long-distance training. I even read a story about a boy from Kansas who was running marathons at the age of six. That, to put it mildly, is too young. One or two miles a day, or even a little more, is okay, but for several reasons I don't believe children should get into the really heavy distance training until they have at least reached their teens. First of all, kids run around plenty as it is in the normal course of their play. Second, preteenagers ought to be using their free time making friends and developing relationships with their family and friends rather than being asked to run X miles a day Y times a week. When these children are old enough to figure out what's happening to them, there's a good chance they'll rebel and be lost to running for the rest of their lives. And if you are thinking that the sooner a child begins to run, the better he or she will get, I can't think of one prominent runner of the past ten years who was a preteen prodigy. Finally, running is hard on certain parts of your body, and it's better for youngsters to wait until they have begun to mature physically before they start running much more than 20 or 25 miles per week.

When it comes to running, kids are natural.

It goes without saying that running is healthy. I don't subscribe to the theory that running prevents heart attacks and strokes and otherwise prolongs life. The medical evidence, while encouraging, is still too shaky and will be until this, the first generation of running boomers, begins to show up in the actuary tables. Either way, it's relatively unimportant. What running does do is improve the quality of life. (I suppose a small argument could be made that running also lengthens it, but if that's true, it is probably because runners tend to smoke less, drink less, and eat more carefully than the rest of the population.) Running reduces your pulse rate, which means your heart is working more efficiently, and it lowers your blood pressure and increases your lung capacity as well.

It also improves your muscle tone and helps you lose weight. Those emaciated runners you see that everybody makes fun of aren't really underweight. They are of *normal* weight, as opposed to being of *average* weight. Get a doctor who knows something about running to show you a height/weight/age chart. You'll find that normal weight is about twenty pounds less than average weight all the way across the board. We Americans are just accustomed to eating too much. I'll have more to say on that score in Chapter 9 on diet and nutrition.

But even a word of caution is necessary about the weight-reducing powers of running. I'll talk about this in more detail later on, but for now let me say that running burns off about 100 calories per mile. So does walking. (It's just that walking takes longer.) That's not very much. But what running does do is burn fat and build muscle—at the same time. Muscle is more dense than fat. Thus, after you have been running for a while, although you won't notice a tremendous reduction in your weight (unless you have also limited your eating, the only real way to diet), you will find that your weight has been redistributed to where it came from in the first place. As I tell women at our clinics, you'll have less jiggle.

Many women worry that a lot of running will make them overly muscular and less feminine, but this won't happen unless it's in your genetic makeup to be that way in the first place. Running improves muscle tone and strength, but only rarely does it increase muscle bulk. It's really nothing to worry about.

It is also pretty obvious that running is a good conditioner for almost every other sport there is. Athletes such as cross-country skiers, cyclists, ice skaters, and soccer players will all benefit from running in their off-seasons. They can use almost the same sets of muscles in nearly the same way. For sports such as tennis, racquetball, squash, baseball, and boxing, where quickness and hand-to-eye coordination are the key factors, running helps build endurance. And if you bowl, play golf, shoot pool, or even drive a race car—relatively sedentary activities on the face of it—a running program will increase your stamina and help you perform more alertly over a longer period of time.

Is there anybody who shouldn't run? In general, the answer is no. But there are certain groups of people who should take precautions before they begin, the largest being men and women over the age of thirty-five who haven't been particularly active for several years. Get a thorough checkup, just to make sure there aren't any surprises lurking around in your body that you didn't know about. If you have a heart condition, or if you have a history of lung disease, diabetes, blood disease, or an orthopedic problem, see a doctor before you begin any sort of exercise program (although running is an excellent way to rebuild weakened or damaged heart muscles following a coronary). But be wary. Not all doctors automatically accept the benefits of running. If one warns you off the sport, get a second opinion and even a third—from a doctor who is himself or herself a runner—before consigning yourself to the sedentary life.

Are you pregnant? Hit the running track. Better yet, start running before you get in the family way. A moderate running program, undertaken with a doctor's guidance, will help keep you in shape and ease the discomforts of your pregnancy. I know of several women who ran well into their second trimester and even their third—and were back out in the streets two or three weeks after they returned from the hospital.

There is one group of people who shouldn't run: those who don't want to. Running isn't for everyone. Some people find it boring, tedious, uninteresting, painful, and otherwise annoying. I do believe that everybody should take up some form of exercise, such as skiing, tennis, or swimming. I don't mind a good hit on the tennis courts myself now and again.

But I urge you to give running a shot. There are many levels of

Pregnancy is no problem.

the game. There are confirmed distance runners like my husband and me, who look forward to our 60 or 70 miles per week and sometimes more. On one side of us are the venture runners and ultramarathoners who think nothing of trotting along for 50 or 60 or even 100 miles at one time, occasionally. On the other side are the men and women who find great benefit from running no more than 30 minutes a day four or five times a week. Regarding competitive running, there are those who would no more think of entering a formal race than flying to the moon. For them, thrice around the block while the soup stock simmers is plenty. Others have the kind of personality that demands a goal of some sort before they can undertake anything. For these men and women who require the dangling carrot, there are all sorts of races available, from short and informal fun runs to organized events at distances up to and beyond the 26.2 miles of the marathon. For now, however, the important thing is to begin.

In summary, running is fun, relaxing, and easy.

The fun part you will eventually discover on your own.

The relaxing part I think I can help you with.

And as far as running being easy goes, consider that you can do it by yourself, you can do it anywhere, and it takes a minimum of time. If you play tennis, you've got to arrange your match, find a court, drive to it, then probably wait awhile for your time to clear. If you play golf, there's the foursome to line up, the inevitable wait at the first tee, and on the weekends it might take you all day to get in your eighteen holes. But if you run, all you have to do is shuck your dress or jeans and slip into your shorts, top, and track shoes, open the door, and take off. No fuss, no muss, and you're back home or back in the office even before you're missed.

Also, running is cheap. All you really need to buy is one pair of good running shoes. There are no greens fees or court costs to worry about, and as for clothing other than footwear, most of the time less is best.

Most encouraging of all, you will improve just by showing up. Unless you are already a world-class runner, your distances will increase and your times will go down in direct proportion to the amount of effort you put into running. That's something that can be said about few other sports in the whole world. People spend a lifetime trying to control a one iron or attempting to master the intricacies of the topspin forehand. Golfers and tennis players at every level, from ranking professionals to weekend duffers, all reach that frustrating point where they know they're just not going to get any better. Not so with running, no matter what your age, sex, or previous condition of flabbiness. Repetition brings improvement and will continue to do so right up until your last run.

I hope this book will be of benefit to runners at nearly every level, but it is written primarily for women who have run a little bit—or have at least thought about it—but perhaps aren't quite sure what to do next.

So let's begin. Twenty-five million of us can't all be wrong.

Choose your running shoes carefully.
Shoes: Brooks Mfg. Co.

3

Outfitting
Yourself

I have only one hard-and-fast rule regarding running equipment: buy a good pair of shoes.

Running begins and ends with your feet, each of which has twenty-six bones and dozens of muscles, ligaments, and tendons all working together in delicate harmony to give you balance, support, and cushioning. They are built to take tremendous punishment, but they're not indestructible. Your feet are connected to your ankles, which are connected to your lower legs, which are connected to your knees, and so on and so forth right up to and including your spine. What happens when your feet hit the ground has a profound, immediate, and cumulative effect on the rest of your body. I would conservatively estimate that three out of every four running aches and pains can be traced to the feet. Pamper yours with the best shoes you can afford.

Don't run in street shoes or even in other kinds of athletic shoes. While a good pair of tennis or sailing shoes won't really hurt you until you've worked up to around 20 miles per week, it's best to let your feet get used to running shoes right from the start. They are lighter than other athletic shoes, and certainly more comfortable. They have to be. Each time you run one mile, your feet hit the ground 1,600 times with a force equal to between two and four times your body weight. No other kind of athletic shoes is designed to take that kind of constant pounding. Tennis shoes, for example, have relatively little padding and are designed to let your feet flex laterally, but in straight-ahead running your primary concerns are cushioning and vertical support. Running in a thin, vertically flexible shoe is courting disaster.

There are basically two kinds of running shoes—racers and trainers. The main differences are that racing shoes are lighter, somewhat flimsier, slightly less comfortable, and occasionally more expensive than training shoes. Racing shoes are built for lightness —a pair of size nines can weigh as little as six ounces compared with nine to twelve ounces for the same size trainer—but unless you're already a world-class distance runner, don't worry about them. Training shoes are easier on your feet, and besides, if you're like me, you won't enjoy running in shoes that haven't been broken in well. When the time comes, you'll do most of your racing in trainers anyway.

As a general rule, you get what you pay for. Comparison shop for shoes just as you would for any other clothing item, but save yourself a lot of time and energy and stay away from cheap imitations of well-known brands. A good pair of shoes costs between $22 and $45. You can certainly pay less, but unless you've lucked into something I haven't heard about, you'll regret your penny pinching in the end. Running shoes often look alike regardless of their quality, but believe me, they're not.

Not too many years ago exactly two manufacturers, Puma and Adidas, had a corner on the running-shoe market, and shopping for a pair was relatively easy. Today more than twenty manufacturers offer in excess of 160 top-of-the-line models from which to choose. To ease the confusion, here are the key points to consider when you're buying your first pair.

Comfort. This goes almost without saying. With their gentle insoles, padded tongues, and soft nylon-and-leather tops, running shoes are pretty comfortable to begin with. But unlike dress shoes, running shoes won't get much more comfortable than they are the day you buy them. Nor will you be able to shuck a pair easily if they begin to irritate your feet in the middle of a run. Carefully check the general feel of the shoe. Does it bind anywhere at all? Are the insoles smooth? Are there any seemingly innocuous defects in workmanship that could cause blisters or chafing during a workout? A couple of years ago a prominent manufacturer came out with a new and very good shoe—except for two small seams that ran from the toe up toward the instep. Runners didn't pay much attention to them, but after several days of running they invariably developed blood blisters beneath their toenails. Properly chagrined, the manufacturer changed the location of the seams and quickly acquired a passel of satisfied customers.

Also, line up your prospective shoes toe to toe and then heel to heel to see if they're evenly balanced. I once traced a severe hip pain to a left shoe that was out of tilt by no more than a quarter of an inch.

Cushioning.   Look at your shoes from the side. They will have a layer of rather firm cushioning between the outer sole and the innersole, the thickness depending on the kind and quantity of material used. They should also have an extra wedge of cushioning that is thickest at the back of your heel and tapers forward beneath your arch almost to the ball of your foot. There are two reasons for this raised heel. Since your heel generally hits the ground first, this is the part of your foot that needs the most protection. Also, by

Comfort and support are your main considerations.

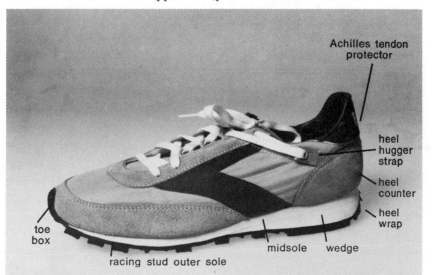

Achilles tendon protector

heel hugger strap

heel counter

heel wrap

toe box

racing stud outer sole

midsole   wedge

Model: Brooks Hugger GT

slightly raising your heel, the cushioning serves to "shorten" your Achilles tendon, relieving this connecting link between your heel and your calf muscles of some of the stress that running inflicts upon it. This raised heel is one of the more obvious distinguishing characteristics of a well-made shoe.

The sole. The outer sole of a running shoe extends up the back of the heel to provide a slightly larger landing area and up the front

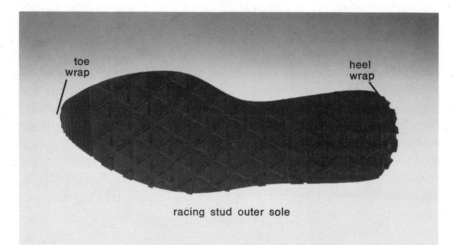

toe wrap

heel wrap

racing stud outer sole

Tread patterns may vary widely from one model to the next.

of the toe to offer a good platform for pushing off. Tread differs greatly from shoe to shoe. Some are flat, with various kinds of designs cut into them. Others have a series of closely placed raised studs that may be triangular, circular, or rectangular. In every case, the purpose is the same—to offer additional cushioning and provide firm traction, especially on hills and trails and during wet weather when any running surface is likely to be slippery.

Flexibility. The outer sole should be slightly wider through the arch and heel than it is through the toes, and much wider than it would be on a dress shoe or another kind of athletic shoe. This is both to spread the impact of your foot plant over the greatest possible area and to give your foot a solid platform. In sports for which you need quick, lateral movement, a flexible shoe with a normally narrow outer sole is necessary to accommodate the many sudden twists and turns of your feet. Not so in running, where your motion is always in one plane. The wide platform of a running shoe helps prevent your foot from turning inward or outward.

Although this outer sole should be quite inflexible, there is a fine line between what is too flexible and what is too stiff. If the shoe is too stiff, you sacrifice comfort; if it's too flexible, you lose the springlike tension the outer sole offers when it unbends as you push off. When in doubt, buy a pair of shoes that seem on the stiff side. It's impossible to stiffen up a shoe that's too flexible, but if your shoes are too stiff, just bend them—toes upward—and jam them overnight in a dresser drawer. That'll loosen things up considerably.

The heel counter. The heel counter is a piece of reinforced leather that wraps around the back of your shoe and keeps your heel from moving too much. Pay particular attention to it if you have narrow heels. Your heel should fit snugly, with only a minimum of lateral movement.

Heel counters occasionally break down quickly. To offset this, some manufacturers have introduced shoes with a lace around the top of them that, when drawn tight, also serves to anchor the heel.

The toe box. Unlike your heel, your toes need all the room they can get. Your foot slides a little every time you take a step. If there's not enough room in the toe box, you'll blister your toes and bruise your toenails in a flash. Check the number of black toes the next time you're around the finish line of a long-distance race. You'll be amazed.

Sometimes women are vain about their feet and try to fit them into shoes that are too small. With dress shoes you can occasionally get away with this; with running shoes you never can. Your toes should have total freedom of movement. You should be able to place your small finger between the tips of your toes and the end of your shoe. More important, be particularly wary of shoes that angle down too sharply from your instep to your toes and don't leave you with plenty of up-and-down room.

If your shoes are too short, there's not much you can do except exchange them. But if they are tapered too sharply, make a vertical incision about an inch long directly over the spot where there's excess pressure. Then make two smaller parallel slits about three-quarters of an inch long on either side. This won't destroy your shoe, and it could save you an expensive return trip to the shoe store.

The arch. Your shoe should have good arch support, but it doesn't have to be elaborate unless you have a problem with that part of your foot. The arch support is usually just a sturdy piece of foam rubber, something that lets your arch know you're thinking about it and to give it a gentle platform to settle down on when you run.

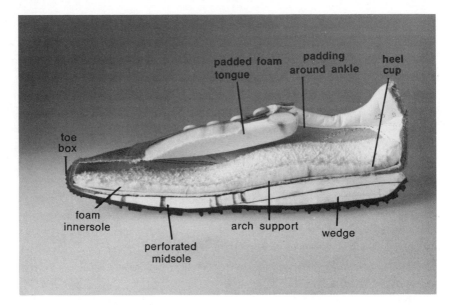

Running shoes may look flimsy, but they're not.

That's a fairly elaborate checklist to keep in mind when you're buying a pair of running shoes, but it's important to take your time. Any decent sporting goods store, and certainly the increasing number of specialty running shops, will offer a wide selection of quality shoes, and sometimes the decision won't be easy. Run around the store for a while in the shoes you've chosen before walking out with them. And don't be lured into choosing the model your friendly salesperson happens to be wearing. Be patient, and be selective.

Running shoes look flimsy, but they're not. Depending on your weight, lightness of step, and several other factors, quality shoes should last between 800 and 1,000 miles before they'll need to be replaced. At a 10-minutes-per-mile pace, that works out to between

130 and 165 hours of running. (Put another way, this means they will carry you through thirty to forty four-hour marathons.)

The tops of your shoes will last forever. What wears out are the soles, particularly the heels, and they should be repaired frequently and carefully to keep them even—and you on an even keel. There are any number of do-it-yourself repair kits on the market. All of them consist of liquid glues or plastics that dry and harden quickly after application.

It is possible to get running shoes resoled with their original tread pattern by sending them off to specialty companies or, if you're lucky, by taking them to a local shoe-repair shop. (There aren't too many, however, that do this kind of work.) While resoling is cheaper than buying a new pair of shoes, I've had a singular lack of success with this. Just as with street shoes, running shoes never quite feel the same after they've been resoled. They bind in new and unexpected places, which can sometimes cause chafing or blisters. Give this a try if you'd like, but don't be surprised if the results are less than satisfying.

I like to have at least two pairs of shoes around in case one set needs repairs, gets wet, or is otherwise knocked out of commission. Like any other kind of footwear, however, no two sets of running shoes are precisely alike, even if they are made by the same manufacturer. Carefully try on shoes every time you buy, and when you find another pair that fits perfectly, latch onto it and guard it with your life.

There are people who acquire running shoes the way stamp collectors collect stamps. Which shoe they use depends on how they feel and the kind of workout they have planned. If, for example, their Achilles tendons feel tight, they might lean to a shoe with a raised heel; for a long workout, a shoe with a lot of cushioning is the answer; if the workout is to be short and intense, perhaps a flatter racing shoe will be chosen.

All this is fine, if you are independently wealthy. Me? I tend to pick my shoes mainly by how well they match up with my running outfit.

If you are having trouble with your feet, there are several things you can do to your shoes to alleviate many minor problems and sometimes a major one.

First, you can play around with your "cookie." The cookie is the piece of foam rubber beneath your arch that's about the size of a rounded half-dollar. By building it up or cutting it down, you can sometimes reduce pain caused by an arch that is either too high or too low.

Another item is the varus wedge, which sits sideways beneath the heel with its higher side under the inside of the heel. Its function is simple. Most runners who make a heel-first foot plant land on the outside of their heels. (So do most people when they walk. Take a look at a pair of your loafers, and you'll see what I mean.) Consequently, a very small area has to absorb a very large shock every time you take a step. Then your foot quickly pronates—rolls inward—until your heel is level with the ground. The varus wedge creates a platform that is tilted more nearly the way your foot is tilted when it strikes the ground. It spreads the impact shock over a greater area and helps reduce pronation.

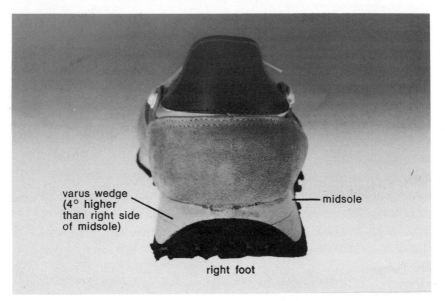

varus wedge
(4° higher
than right side
of midsole)

midsole

right foot

Some shoes have a varus wedge built into them.

At least one company, Brooks, builds a patented four-degree varus wedge into certain models of its shoes, but you can achieve the same effect by gluing a small section of foot padding to the insole on the inside half of your heel.

Then, of course, there is the common foot pad, of the kind Dr. Scholl made famous, which adds cushioning and arch support. If you try a foot pad, however, remove the existing cookie from your shoe. With both the cookie and the pad in your shoe, you'll have too much of a good thing.

These and other orthotics—an orthotic, in simplest terms, being any kind of foot support—are fine for runners who need them. But don't experiment unless you're sure they'll be of some help. As the saying goes, "If the machine ain't broke, don't fix it."

Finally, it seems as though every few weeks one manufacturer or another comes out with a new shoe or upgrades an old one. Well and good, but don't rush out to buy it until it's been tested in the marketplace—by somebody else. Many of the changes are only cosmetic, and occasionally a new design just doesn't work right. Wait about six months to see what kind of reception the new shoe gets or until it has been judged by a publication such as *Runner's World,* which once a year rates most of the top-line shoes for the benefit of its subscribers.

For years, distance runners seemed to enjoy dressing down. The runner's "uniform" was a million-dollar pair of shoes, a top, and a ten-cent pair of shorts, the grungier and scruffier the better. (I began in a pair of cutoff jeans and a checkerboard shirt I wore in my sorority's washboard band.) But one of the nicer side effects of the running boom has been that clothing manufacturers have learned how to make quite fashionable running gear. Several top runners, including myself, are associated with some of these companies and have helped market clothing that is both functional and attractive. The variety of designer shorts, shirts, socks, warm-up suits, and the like and the stunning colors in which they come are a pleasant change from the old days. While some of the designer-influenced clothing might be considered hype, on the whole it's a nice hype. There's nothing wrong with looking good when you run. Occasionally, though, you'll find that manufacturers have let the designers take the upper hand. The end product of this confusion of chic and function is rarely a disaster, except to your pocketbook, but it occasionally can be annoying. For runners, the bottom line is comfort and function.

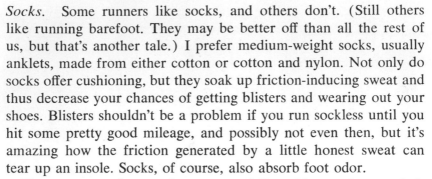

Socks. Some runners like socks, and others don't. (Still others like running barefoot. They may be better off than all the rest of us, but that's another tale.) I prefer medium-weight socks, usually anklets, made from either cotton or cotton and nylon. Not only do socks offer cushioning, but they soak up friction-inducing sweat and thus decrease your chances of getting blisters and wearing out your shoes. Blisters shouldn't be a problem if you run sockless until you hit some pretty good mileage, and possibly not even then, but it's amazing how the friction generated by a little honest sweat can tear up an insole. Socks, of course, also absorb foot odor.

If you wear socks, put them on carefully—this may be too obvious to mention, but I will anyway—and no wrinkles, please. At worst, you'll court blisters if your sock gets squinched inside your shoe. At best, you'll annoy yourself by having to stop and straighten them out.

Shorts. Running shorts should fit loosely, grabbing you gently around the waist with the aid of an elastic band or a drawstring, and nowhere else. They should be loose across your buttocks and through your crotch. I like the kind with a slight slit up the side. Shorts that are too tight—anywhere—restrict your freedom of movement and promote chafing. Similarly, 100 percent nylon shorts are better than those made of cotton or even cotton and polyester. They cling less. Rather than wear a pair of panties, I prefer shorts with a cotton inner liner. (Both men's and women's shorts come with or without.) Finally, make sure your shorts have a pocket, one you can securely close.

Tops. Any old T-shirt will do, although for maximum coolness and all-around comfort, I like a runner's singlet that is 50 percent polyester and 50 percent cotton. Sleeves, of course, are fine, but check for tightness through your shoulders and chest and beneath your arms. This is the one garment where fashion most often gets in the way of function and comfort.

Bras. I recommend one—at the very least a tank top or a body suit—because there is some medical evidence that running as well as other kinds of exercise breaks down breast tissue and causes sagging. Whether or not this is true, I'm more comfortable with a bra than without. The only benefits of bouncing breasts are those that accrue to the spectators. The running bras that have come onto the market during the past couple of years are a definite improvement over what used to be available. They're softer, have hidden seams (or outside seams) to reduce chafing, offer great support, and some of them are fashionable enough to be used as running tops by themselves.

Warm-up suits. I like warm-up suits. I have something of a weakness for them, in fact, although this is another item sometimes victimized by overzealous designers. Make sure your warm-up suit (or suits) is loose-fitting and opens easily at the neck, wrists, and ankles so that you can control ventilation. Further, make sure the legs are pegged, or at least gathered at the ankles. Many of today's suits have fashionably flared legs, and while they look good as you stand around the patio, they simply get in the way when you try to work out in them.

Warm-up suits are usually both functional and fashionable.

All these items should be made from lightweight fabrics that are breathable and easily washable, which, as I've suggested, means synthetics, cotton, or cotton with polyester. Cotton is the best heat conductor among the natural fibers, while the polyesters and other synthetics add durability and reduce wrinkling.

Beyond these basics, there are a score or more of auxiliary items—gadgets, almost—that you can take along with you if you choose. And that, if you did, would add another ten pounds to your weight. A casual glance at any running publication will reveal an awesome variety of things: pedometers to measure how far you've run and stopwatches to record how fast; short aluminum nightsticks and small cans of Mace to ward off attackers of either the human or the animal variety; runners' jewelry and runners' identification cards. And of course, you can get a lightweight pouch in which to carry all this stuff. If any of these items appeals to you, go ahead and buy it; but these are obviously not mandatory issue.

In addition to the basic clothing, what I usually wear during my runs are a sweatband and a visor. I wear the sweatband around my wrist and use it to wipe the perspiration out of my eyes. (If it's very hot, I'll also use a headband.) I wear a visor because I have light-sensitive eyes and no product of which I am aware has yet been invented that satisfactorily holds sunglasses (or any other kinds of glasses) in place during a workout.

I do carry the aforementioned can of Mace. It doesn't weigh but a couple of ounces and fits snugly in the palm of my hand. I've never been mugged while running, but I know women who have, and sometimes dogs and I just don't get along together.

Last, don't forget the house key—and if you so desire, you can buy a little key holder that attaches to the laces of your shoe.

You'll want to modify your equipment according to the weather, and for when you run at dusk or in the dark. Here's how.

Heat.   Between 1970 and 1975 I won the Peachtree Road Race the five times I entered it. The reason I didn't make it a perfect six for six in '76 was that I collapsed, the victim of heat prostration. I was chugging along in fine shape until I reached the halfway point. Then my skin began to tingle, and I started to feel faint.

The next thing I was aware of was falling into a fire hydrant by the side of the road. I grinned at a policeman who tried to help me and babbled, "Oh, sir, don't worry about me. I do this all the time."

I was, of course, delirious—even more, I soon found out, than I had imagined. I figured I had fallen at the moment I began to get dizzy. I was shocked and scared to learn my accident had taken place within 250 yards of the finish line. I had run totally blanked out for more than 3 miles.

Heat and humidity are the number one enemies of a runner. As far as equipment goes, there's very little you can do, considering you're already wearing only as much as modesty and common sense dictate. But there are a few ways to make hot-weather running a little more bearable.

Don't put anything on your head unless you're bald and worried about sunburn. Wear a visor, not a hat, if you want to keep the sun out of your eyes. You lose 40 percent of your body heat through your head and hands. Keep them uncovered.

Wear clothing that is white, or light-colored, to help reflect the heat.

Drink plenty of fluids both before and after your run, and know where there are drinking fountains or one or two friendly sprinklers along your route. Your body is usually pretty good at telling you what it needs—except when it comes to liquids. You won't drink nearly the amount of fluids you lose during a run unless you force yourself, so toss down an extra glass of water or fruit juice a half-hour before you start your workout (it will take that long for it to enter your system) and again after you've completed it.

Run early in the morning, if possible, or late in the evening in order to miss the most brutal heat of the day.

Finally, if both the temperature and humidity are above 85, don't run at all. These figures are somewhat arbitrary—medical authorities disagree on the absolute danger levels—but there is a point at which the heat and humidity in combination make exercise dangerous for even the best-conditioned athlete.

Cold.   Dress in thin layers rather than in one thick layer. Air is a great insulator, and when it is trapped between your various layers of clothing, it will help keep you warm. Also, several layers of thin clothing absorb sweat better than one heavy sweat shirt.

Let common sense determine the number of layers. On an average cold day I might start with a T-shirt, cover it with a turtleneck, add another T-shirt, and if necessary finish with a thin windbreaker of some sort.

Just as you want your body heat to escape on a hot day, you want to retain it on a nippy one. Wear a hat and a pair of gloves because heat escapes from your head and hands first.

Down below, I can usually get by with shorts and knee socks. Your legs won't be uncomfortable except in the bitterest temperatures, and in fact, the only reason I even wear knee socks is to keep my calf muscles from tightening up.

Don't overdress. Dress to accommodate how you'll feel once you've been running 5 to 7 minutes, not how cold you are at the start. You *will* warm up, and it's better to be slightly uncomfortable for a few minutes early on than to be overly hot during the remainder of your workout with no opportunity to shed your extra clothing.

Wind. Although there are some days when it's too hot and humid to run, it's never too cold—as long as there's no wind. Even then, wind is not dangerous unless the temperature is well below freezing. Whether or not you can run safely is up to the wind-chill factor, a numerical description of the effects of cold air in combination with wind. If the wind-chill factor is below −72, it's dangerously cold, but not until then.

If you're going to have to run with the wind in your face at some point, plan to do it during the first half of your workout so that you can finish with the breeze at your back. Letting the wind push you home is a pleasant way to end a blustery run, and you're less likely to get chilled.

My experience with cold-weather running is somewhat limited. In Atlanta it rarely stays below freezing for an entire day, and if the temperature dips to zero, the city pretty much closes down. So I asked my friend Jess Bell what to do when it *really* gets cold. He lives near Cleveland and has run through several of those brutal Great Lakes winters with a minimum of difficulty.

"We've had some cracking cold days up here," Jess said, "but my wife, Julie, and I have never found a day when we couldn't run, although if the temperature drops below minus twenty-five, we might wait until it warms up. We dress strictly by the layer system. I wear a T-shirt, a turtleneck, and a sweat shirt, and then a wind jacket of some kind, usually a nylon shell. They're light, and they don't restrict your movement. I also wear shorts and long underwear—regular long johns if it's down around zero and thermal underwear when it's supercold.

"I wear mittens, not gloves, because with mittens you can ball up your hands, and they stay much warmer that way. If that's not good enough, I might wear thin gloves beneath the mittens. You don't need heavy ones. All you'll do is sweat a lot.

"I wear a hat, of course, but not a wool hat. I prefer something lighter, made of a material like Orlon. Sometimes just a baseball cap will do—anything to keep me from losing too much heat.

"Finally, I wear a scarf to throw over my face if the wind whips up, one made of silk or some kind of synthetic. Balaclavas and ski masks are too much. Your breath condenses on them, and pretty soon the buildup of frost is more of a problem than running without anything on your face would have been. Breathing cold air, incidentally, even supercold air, is no problem. Your body warms it up sufficiently long before it reaches your lungs.

"The one difficulty we have up here is slipping and sliding on ice and hard-packed snow. I've talked to at least one shoe manufacturer about making a spiked running shoe for winter, but no luck so far. What I did find was a set of spikes in one of those marvelous L. L. Bean catalogues. You just strap them onto your running shoes the same way mountain climbers use crampons. The spikes are short, of hard steel, and set in rubber so they won't come through your shoe. They're for working around the farm. They come in small, medium, and large, and they're great."

Running at night. Only one point needs to be made about this: wear some sort of reflecting device to warn cars and other vehicles of your presence. Some runners prefer a full reflecting vest similar to the kind school guards use. Others like to wear running tops and bottoms with reflecting stripes built into their design. At the very least, buy a roll of reflecting tape and do up your shorts and tops yourself, front and back. You'll be glad you did. Accidents can happen to anybody, even the most wary and experienced runners.

4

Relaxing into Your Own Natural Style

Your ultimate running goal is to cover the greatest possible distance in the fastest possible time while using the least amount of energy. Unlike most things in life, this is easier done than said.

Any discussion of running technique begins with your feet. Running is an extension of walking. When you walk, you land on your heels, roll up over the balls of your feet, and push off with your toes. When you do this energetically enough, so that you briefly glide through the air between steps, you are copying the rolling heel-and-toe gait favored by most casual joggers and many world-class marathoners as well.

But not all of them. In fact, there seems to be a trend among the better distance runners to land more up on the balls of their feet, with their heels slapping the ground only briefly and delicately on each step. Bill Rodgers, who is currently the world's best marathoner, favors this technique, and on occasion so do I. When you begin to run, one of these styles will no doubt feel more natural than the other. If not, experiment with both, and stick with the one that you find more comfortable. You'll get the job done either way.

As you walk, your left and right feet generally make two separate and parallel tracks. When you run, however, the natural twisting of your body will make your footfall more nearly Indian file so that you will plant each step almost directly in front of the

Bill Rodgers, whose style is to land well up on the balls of his feet, in 1979 won his third Boston Marathon in five years.

others. This is perfectly acceptable as long as your feet don't actually cross over each other. If they do, take it as a sign that you are twisting your body too much and try to reduce your swivel. An easy way to check on this is to run on hard sand, down a lane divider at a running track, or along a painted line in the middle of the street (assuming, of course, there's no traffic) and notice for yourself exactly what your footfall looks and feels like.

Ideally, your feet should point straight ahead when you land on them, but if you are slightly pigeon-toed or splayfooted, don't worry about a thing. By attempting to change this aspect of your foot plant, you'll do more harm than good to the delicate system of muscles, bones, tendons, ligaments, and joints that make up your lower legs.

Tom Fleming finished fourth at Boston in 1979.

Kate Shea (left) and Martha White look like they're floating—
think light and you'll run light.

What I am saying is that no two footfalls are exactly the same,
nor should they be. But no matter how you make your foot plant,
it is of fundamental importance that you learn to make it *lightly*.
The best runners, whatever their size and shape, don't run at all—
they float. They give the impression that they could run over eggs
and not crack a single one, so light is their step.

In order to *run* lightly, you must *think* lightly. Imagine that your
body is without weight, like a feather, or that you are running on
a thin sheet of ice which you don't want to break because beneath
it is a deep body of very cold water. Another trick is to think of
your feet as cat's paws. Every time you land on the ground, grab
at it and gently but firmly pull yourself forward. This may require
some mental gymnastics on your part (I told you running is easier
done than said), but a lot of running is mental, and it does work.
Trust me.

A more concrete way to run lightly is to shorten your stride. If beginning runners have a common fault, it is a tendency to overstride. They think that a long, loping stride automatically means a more powerful stride, but that's not necessarily true. You generate power only when you push off your toes, not while you're flying through the air, and an overly long stride results in a bouncing gait that is jarring on your legs and needlessly inefficient. Take short, choppy strides, even if at first you think they are too short and too choppy. They'll help you float. Lightly.

Precisely how long should your stride be? I am asked this question almost daily, but in all honesty I haven't the slightest idea. I don't even know what mine should be or what, in fact, it is. Probably a distance equal to two-thirds of your height is about right—that is, if you are six feet tall, you should be hitting the ground every four feet or so—but that's only a guess. Several years ago a group of experienced runners was tested at Penn State University. Each runner's stride was measured and compared with his or her mathematically calculated ideal. Almost without exception, the actual length of each runner's stride was within a few percentage points of his or her projected ideal. The point? That you will develop your optimal stride length naturally. It's another part of running technique that you never have to worry about.

Frank Shorter gave American running a big boost with his marathon victory at the Munich Olympics in 1972.

Ben and I opening it up during a training run.

The next part of your body to consider is your hips. There is a tendency among some runners at every level to run slightly bent over at the waist, as though they were carrying the weight of the world on their shoulders. The best way to run, however, is with your hips thrust forward. This accomplishes several things. It keeps your back erect and perpendicular to the ground, reducing the tension along your spinal column. It places your upper body weight directly above your waist and buttocks, where it belongs, eliminating the stress on your thighs. It prevents your chest and stomach from squinching up, allowing you to breathe easily and comfortably. It keeps your head held high and your eyes firmly planted far down the road, easing much of the tightness throughout your upper body, especially in your neck and shoulders. Finally, it gives you a nice psychological boost. It's as though somebody had attached a rope to your midriff and were literally pulling you down the road.

Next, your arms. Think of your body as a car, with your legs being the wheels and your arms the motor. (I first heard this analogy several years ago, and it's a good one.) Obviously your legs can move without any help at all from your arms, but they—your arms—are going to swing along naturally anyway, just like they do when you walk, and you might as well put them to good use. When I sometimes get tired and start floundering around a little bit, I tell myself that if I can just keep my motor—my arms—pumping, then my wheels—my legs—will have to continue churning no matter what. This is another mental trick, but it does help, especially during a race or if you are doing strenuous hill work.

The pumping of your arms acts as a gyroscope for the rest of your body. It counterbalances the swing of your legs and helps control the movement of your upper body. Your forward arm swing should never cross the center of your chest, and your backswing should never extend much beyond your hips. If your swing is too long or wild in either direction, your shoulders will start to twist, and you'll soon lose your rhythm entirely. You want to keep all the parts of your body moving forward in as straight a line as possible, and the best way to ensure this is to keep firm control of your arms.

Bend your arms so that your hands are about stomach-high. Keep your fists closed, but not clenched. You want to be as loose and as relaxed as possible, at all times and under every conceivable condition. On your first few runs, you may find that your hands almost involuntarily clench up into tight little balls at the first hint of fatigue. This is also the first sign of tension, and the easiest way to get relaxed again is simply to unclench those fists. I can't promise that the fatigue will go away when you do this, but running relaxed will make it more bearable. I often take this idea one step further and drop my arms to my sides in the middle of a run and shake them vigorously. This loosens all my muscles, not only in my hands and arms but in my neck, shoulders, and torso as well.

Now let's consider your breathing. As strange as this may sound, given the involuntary nature of the act, many runners, and most other people as well, don't breathe correctly. They breathe with their chests, taking shallow, tight, inefficient breaths that don't begin to let their bodies utilize all the available oxygen. The correct way to breathe is to inhale air all the way down into your abdomen, so that your tummy literally heaves with the effort. This is called belly breathing, a technique taught in yoga classes. (It is also the way you breathe as you sleep, when your body is totally relaxed and thus operating most efficiently.) Learning to breathe this way will take a little bit of practice, but it's well worth the effort. To test yourself, lie on your back, and place a book on your stomach. If the book doesn't move very much as you breathe, you're breathing too shallowly. Concentrate on getting air down into your stomach until that book is on an elevator every time you inhale and exhale.

There is another point about breathing that may be obvious, but perhaps not. At rest, you no doubt breathe through your nose or through your mouth. One or the other—probably your nose unless you have a cold—but not both. No problem. But if for some reason you're unable to breathe through your mouth *and* your nose when you run, you'll suffer mightily. If you don't believe me, try running sometime with your mouth closed or your nose pinched. This is one reason, among others, why you should never run when you have a severe cold. You just can't suck in enough oxygen.

Synchronize your breathing with the steps you take. This is another part of running that usually happens naturally. But not always—especially when you're tired or if you suddenly hit a patch of uneven ground. The way to breathe with the most efficiency and control is to inhale every second, third, fourth, fifth, or sixth step—whatever. The frequency of your breathing isn't terribly significant. The important thing is to breathe rhythmically and not to take sudden, cramped half-breaths in mid-stride.

Finally, and most importantly, *relax.* I cannot emphasize this enough. Nothing defeats a runner so much as muscular tension, and you should strive to avoid it at all costs. I have already suggested two ways—by unclenching your hands and shaking out your arms. Another way is mental. As you run, concentrate on specific parts of your body, all the way from your neck and shoulders down to your toes, and if you sense that one of them is not loose and relaxed, focus your mind on it, and think *limp* until it is. Running while you are tense not only is physically wearing but can be mentally debilitating as well. It will exhaust you as quickly as any hill you are ever likely to run across.

What we have accumulated so far is a checklist for runners:

- Whether you run with a rolling heel-and-toe gait or up on the balls of your feet, think *light.*
- Take shorter strides than you feel you should. In time, you will acquire your ideal stride length; for now it is important not to overstride.
- Thrust your hips forward.

• Keep your back straight and perpendicular to the ground, with your upper body weight directly over your waist and buttocks.

• Keep your torso pointed squarely in front of you. Don't twist it.

• Hold your head high, and plant your eyes far down the road.

• Hold your hands stomach-high.

• Keep your arm swing short and compact. Don't let your forward swing cross the center of your body or your backswing extend much beyond your hips.

• Breathe rhythmically, in time with your steps.

• *Relax.*

Now forget everything I've said for a moment.

Take a close look at the six men and women pictured on these pages. They all are talented and accomplished world-class runners who have been in training for years, some of them under the tutelage of the very best coaches in the world. You might think that by now they would all pretty much run the same way and that their styles would be very close to the ideal I've just described. But as you can easily tell, nothing could be further from the truth. And if you have ever seen the best runners in action, either in person or on film, you realize that no two of them, men or women, do everything in exactly the same way. Some run with their hands

Even at the top, no two runners have exactly the same style.

Miki Gorman

Nina Kuscsik

Laura Cravens

Chris Stewart

clutched to their chests while others almost dangle them at their sides. I know runners who hold their heads high and others who stare at the ground as if they'd just discovered the reason for pooper-scoopers. Some are classically graceful from the waist down but twist their upper bodies as though they were on a disco dance floor. Others look fine from the waist up—their posture is perfect, and nothing swings from side to side—but take little mincing steps that are painful even to contemplate. One particularly fine runner, Mary Shea, caught up in the intensity of a race sometimes carries her right arm up near her neck somewhere, like a bird with a broken wing.

Is there anything wrong with all this variety? Absolutely not. I wouldn't tinker with any of these runners' styles for the world. (Certainly not Shea's. She set the American record for the women's 10,000-meter run at the 1979 Amateur Athletic Union outdoor track and field championships.) And if I had the opportunity to watch you run, I probably wouldn't make too many suggestions about your running style either.

In most cases, style is nothing more than a body's way of accommodating and compensating for its uniqueness. For example, women with flared hips often cannot run without some twisting of their torso. People who are naturally pigeon-toed, as I have said, will find that running puts undue stress on their lower legs if their feet are pointed straight in front of them. If you have never played sports before, or if you have laid off them for several years, the muscles and tendons that support your knees probably will be very weak, and you'll find yourself running almost knock-kneed. The illustrations are endless. People come in all sizes, shapes, and ages, and these determine how they will look on the running track.

Technique is just not that important in distance running. This is true at every level, and especially for beginners, who in most other sports must have at least a slight mastery of certain fundamentals before they can begin to enjoy whatever it is they're trying to do. And technique is absolutely crucial for track and field athletes such as sprinters, who have little margin for error because they must accomplish their tasks in such a short amount of time. But as a distance runner you are doing something that is natural, you are always operating well within your physical limits—or should be—and you literally have all day to reach your goals.

If you give yourself half the chance, you will develop a style best suited to your own physique almost without realizing it. This is precisely what happened to Joanne Woodward, the actress, during the filming of the 1978 television movie *See How They Run*. The story is about an unathletic New England housewife who becomes obsessed with the Boston Marathon. She is determined to run in it and to complete the course, and with great difficulty, she does. (Shades of my 1972 Peach Bowl Marathon run.) Woodward took up running to prepare for her role in the spring of 1977, and at the end of a month she was up to a gentle mile or so per workout. Then she went to Boston to be filmed in the middle of the mad pack at the start of the real Boston Marathon. With the cameras grinding, she jogged her mile and dropped out. The filming of various race sequences continued over the next couple of months, during which time Woodward continued to run and built herself up to 2 or 3 miles per workout.

Then everybody went to the editing room to piece the whole thing together. Woodward was shocked. The last of her running takes bore absolutely no resemblance to the first—it was like watching two different runners. The expensive result was that the film crew had to assemble a ton of extras and reshoot the start of the race entirely.

Pretty much on her own and without really thinking about it, Woodward had developed a graceful, fluid, and efficient running style, a style that best accommodated her individual physiology. Which is precisely what will happen to you.

If you are going to acquire your running style naturally, what is the point of my checklist? There are two reasons for it.

First, it is there to give you a few things to think about. In running, as in most other sports, rhythm is everything. Each single part of running technique relates directly to the rest, and if you are able to do just one of these fundamentals correctly, the rest will follow. Just as a tennis player or a golfer needs a checklist to help regain his or her rhythm when shots begin to go astray, so too does a runner. If you find you are running awkwardly and out of sync, pick one item on the list, and concentrate on it and it alone for a while. You'll be pleasantly surprised by how easily your rhythm returns and how quickly everything else falls into place.

Second, despite the infinite variety of running styles, there *is* a correct way to run. Some quirks in technique are merely cosmetic and best left alone, but others can be harmful and, once learned, are mighty hard to get rid of. So work hard, and give yourself at least three months to achieve the ideal. But at the same time use my checklist as a guide, not as a bible, and don't worry too much if you acquire some stylistic peculiarities of your own. You'll come pretty close to what's right for you just by showing up.

I implied earlier that I'm not particularly fond of running charts, graphs, timetables—anything that smacks of regimentation—and that's still true. When you are starting out, however, some sort of formal program is necessary and even desirable. So let me give you my three-month training schedule for beginning runners, talk about it a little bit, and explain how it can be modified to suit your individual goals.

Schedule I
Do each workout four times during the week listed.

Week One
Walk 20 minutes.

Day	
1	____
2	____
3	____
4	____

Week Two
Walk 30 minutes.

Day	
1	____
2	____
3	____
4	____

Week Three
Run 2 minutes, walk 4 minutes.   Day
Do this sequence five times.
                                         ———————————

                                         1   ————

                                         2   ————

                                         3   ————

                                         4   ————

Week Four
Run 3 minutes, walk 3 minutes,   Day
and repeat this four times.
                                         ———————————

                                         1   ————

                                         2   ————

                                         3   ————

                                         4   ————

Week Five
Run 5 minutes, walk 2.5 minutes,   Day
and repeat four times.
                                         ———————————

                                         1   ————

                                         2   ————

                                         3   ————

                                         4   ————

Week Six
Run 7 minutes, walk 3 minutes,   Day
and repeat two times.
                                         ———————————

                                         1   ————

                                         2   ————

                                         3   ————

                                         4   ————

Week Seven
Run 8 minutes, walk 2 minutes,
and repeat two times.

Day

1 ——

2 ——

3 ——

4 ——

Week Eight
Run 9 minutes, walk 2 minutes,
and repeat once more,
then run 8 minutes.

Day

1 ——

2 ——

3 ——

4 ——

Week Nine
Run 9 minutes, walk 1 minute,
and repeat two times.

Day

1 ——

2 ——

3 ——

4 ——

Week Ten
Run 13 minutes, walk 2 minutes,
and repeat once.

Day

1 ——

2 ——

3 ——

4 ——

Week Eleven
Run 14 minutes, walk 1 minute,
and repeat once.

Day	
1	___
2	___
3	___
4	___

Week Twelve
Run 14 minutes, walk 1 minute,
and repeat once. (This schedule
is the same as for Week Eleven.)

Day	
1	___
2	___
3	___
4	___

Week Thirteen
Run 30 minutes.

Day	
1	___
2	___
3	___
4	___

My schedule is simple and straightforward and incorporates
several ideas that will help you enjoy running right from the start.

Why is it of three months' duration? Obviously, the time is somewhat arbitrary. The schedule could just as easily be two months,
four months, or even six months long. But I've found that it takes
most beginners about that long to find out whether they like running.

Running is not for everyone, as I've suggested, and it might not be for you. Even if it is, there's no point in making the sometimes difficult transition from nonrunner to runner any harder than it has to be. If you are convinced of the benefits of running and are pretty sure you'll like it, just block out those 20 or 30 minutes in your schedule and find out for yourself. In thirteen weeks you will at least be satisfied that you've given running a fair trial, whether or not you stay with it. I think you will.

Notice that all I'm asking you to do during the first two weeks is take a walk. Some of you may think this is a waste of time, that if Gayle Barron is trying to convince folks to run, why doesn't she just tell them to go out and run? A good question.

One of the keys to any successful running program is regularity, and perhaps the hardest single thing for a beginning runner to do is accept running as a habit. It does you very little good to run five days in a row, lay off for two weeks, and then start up again. You won't see any improvement, but you will wind up repeating the same short, frustrating cycle until you give up running entirely. It happens all the time.

It's the easiest thing in the world to find an excuse not to run: Your kids are squawking, you didn't get home from the office on time and it's getting dark outside, it's raining, you've got a dinner party to prepare for, and so on and so forth. I've heard them all, and if the truth be told, I've got a few of my own stashed away that *you've* probably never heard before.

But it's pretty hard to rationalize not taking a 20- or 30-minute *walk* four times a week, and what this does is get you in the habit of blocking out that short bit of time so that when you do start running, your workouts will be as automatic as all the other routine things you do during the day. Trick yourself if you have to. Park your car 20 or 30 minutes away from your office or the drugstore when you're headed that way. (Yes, I know you've got to get back. Take the bus—or walk.)

Besides, a good, brisk walk several times a week isn't bad exercise in itself. It's not as good as running, but it's certainly better than nothing.

One of the more amusing discussions in running circles is over the best time of day to work out. My advice is, simply, run whenever your body feels like it.

There are morning people, and there are evening people. Just as your mind no doubt works best at certain times of the day, so does your body. Listen to it, and it will tell you a lot. Most studies have shown that the human body functions best in the late afternoon, between the hours of four and six o'clock. It's loose and relaxed, and the day's fatigue hasn't yet begun to set in. Mine fits that category. I most enjoy my running then—and I'm certainly not a morning person. After eight hours' sleep I'm generally pretty creaky.

But not everybody can run at the same time, nor should everyone. If your job keeps you on your feet all day or is otherwise physically demanding, you might be better off taking your workout in the morning. If you have a household to maintain and a car pool to worry about, you might find that 30 minutes in midday best suits your schedule.

This is something you'll have to work out on your own. If you have the luxury of time, experiment. I knew of one runner in Chicago who felt she always had to run at the crack of dawn. Well, it gets very cold in Chicago sometimes, and she had a slightly gimpy knee, the result of an old skiing accident. After a month of running, the combination of the lousy weather and her tight morning muscles began to take its toll. Her knee hurt so badly she could hardly walk—let alone run—although she followed the book and applied heat to her injury before her workouts and ice to it afterward. Then she started running in the afternoons. In a few weeks the pain went away, and she was enjoying her runs as she never before could. The slightly warmer air and her normal day's activities limbered up her legs just enough to relieve the tightness in her bad knee.

As for what days of the week to run on, any four will do. I wouldn't, however, recommend running on four consecutive days. Rather, space your workouts throughout the week to give your body a chance to recover. Something like a Tuesday-Thursday-Saturday-Sunday schedule is best, but if you have to miss a scheduled run, don't fret. Make it up on one of your off days.

Remember, one of your main objectives during these three months is to get used to the idea of working out regularly, without having vacations, business trips, bad weather, and other convenient excuses interfere with your program. The idea is for your running to become a habit, even addictive. Then you will have made the first breakthrough: you will look forward to running with pleasure, rather than consider it a burden perhaps to be cast aside at the first opportunity. This won't necessarily happen automatically. It will require a lot of willpower, especially in the beginning.

Whenever possible, confine your running to flat surfaces during these first months. This will be easy if you live in Kansas; more difficult if your home is in the Poconos, but give it a shot anyway. There will be plenty of time later on to experience the joys and agonies of the hills.

There are actually three good reasons for staying on the flat. The first relates to one of the basic purposes of this schedule—to get you used to working out regularly for a specific period of time. When you start running up and down things or even along rolling terrain, you will probably get it in your head that 5 minutes of hill work takes as much out of you, say, as 8 minutes on the flat, and you will no doubt be right. But you might also then have the inclination to cut short your workout by several minutes. That would be a mistake.

Second, during these first months you will be subconsciously learning how to pace yourself. Experienced runners have clocks in their heads. They know precisely how long they have been on the road and exactly how far they have traveled. Hills tend to throw off your inner clock.

Third, you will also be subconsciously learning how to listen to your body. This is a rather subtle thought, and I'll talk about it in detail later on. For now, just let me say it is sometimes difficult to monitor your body while you are doing hill work. By staying on a flat surface, you can more easily establish the standards against which you will eventually be able to judge accurately the many changes your body goes through as you run.

So for now, find a good running track—the kind with a rubberized surface is best if there's one handy—or stick to level roads. In the long run, you'll be better off.

Perhaps you are surprised to find no mention of distance in my schedule. This is because distance is relatively unimportant in distance running. For beginners, and for intermediates and advanced runners as well, it's not how far you run but the amount of time you spend running that counts. (Indeed, maybe the sport ought to be called time running.)

The emphasis that runners place on accumulating their mileage is unfortunate and often self-defeating. If one runner does 5 miles in 30 minutes, and another only 3, who is to say which one had the better workout? Certainly the first runner is faster, but it is likely that both benefited equally—when the benefit is measured against their individual capacities. And if two runners each do 3 miles, the first in 20 minutes and the second in 30, there is no question but that the second runner has achieved more simply because she's been out there longer.

There is, however, an obvious correlation between time and distance, and I would be a liar if I said I didn't think in terms of distance myself. (But that is because I have a pretty good clock in my head and know how fast I run. Most of the time, when I begin a workout, I plan to run a certain number of minutes and let the distance take care of itself.) Most people do like to know how far they've run. The schedule assumes you can walk 1 mile in 20 minutes, and as a beginner you can run 1 mile in 10 minutes. This varies from individual to individual, but if you hit these marks, you will progress from 4 miles per week of walking to 12 miles per week of running during these three months.

Whatever your speed, run at your own pace and well within your capacity. A runner's gimmick called the Talk Test can help you judge this. It was devised years ago by Bill Bowerman, the former track coach at the University of Oregon, and it's just what the name implies. Whenever you run and no matter for how long, maintain a pace slow enough to allow you to carry on a conversation. If you can run and talk at the same time, you are running well within yourself and will always have something in reserve. Again—and again and again—the object in distance running is not to work yourself into a state of exhaustion, but very gradually to increase your tolerance and capacity to the point where you can run as fast and as far as your own individual body will let you. It doesn't do you any good, mentally or physically, to end a workout in a state of near collapse with your skin all prickly and your heart racing away like there's no tomorrow.

There is one important qualification to the Talk Test, however, because of the physiological phenomenon known as second wind. It seems to take most runners anywhere from 5 to 7 minutes of good, steady jogging before their hearts, lungs, and muscles all get to working efficiently. When I run, I huff and puff like crazy for the first few minutes. I can't get my rhythm or my breath, and I certainly can't talk. But almost precisely at the first mile mark, which for me is 6 to 7 minutes into my workout, I break out into a good sweat, my heart rate steadies, my lungs feel like they're working right, and Ben, or whomever it is I'm running with, and I can then start our conversation. It's almost like your body says, *Okay, you've got me out here, and we're not going home anytime soon, so we might as well make the best of it.* That is your second wind.

You won't run enough consecutive minutes to experience your second wind until well into your second month. Be on the lookout for it around Week Seven or Week Eight, when you are running 8 or 9 minutes before your first breather. Not only will your second wind feel good, but it's also a solid indication that you're making progress.

Don't expect miracles. My schedule doesn't provide for any. If it seems slow and leisurely and appears to stress underachievement, it's because it is doing just that. There is no worse feeling than to leave your workout on the track, and no easier way to get turned off by the sport. Runners at every level are guilty of this, but it's one habit you can break even before you acquire it.

It took me three months—back in the Dark Ages—to work up to where I could run a mile without stopping, and I stayed at that plateau for two years. I certainly could have moved along more quickly if I'd had any real idea what I was doing out there. But I'm often glad that I didn't progress more rapidly. My slow start, however unwitting, gave me a solid foundation that has let me enjoy running for fourteen years. If I were starting today, I'm not sure I could resist the peer pressure to do too much too soon.

You'll no doubt feel that pressure yourself. You'll bump into somebody at a cocktail party, for instance, who will casually mention that she's doing 5 miles per day after only a couple of months of training, and you'll be tempted to step up your own schedule. Be wary. Don't compare yourself to others. You've got your own body to worry about, not your friend's or neighbor's.

However, feel free to play around a little. Like my earlier check-list, my schedule is a guideline, not gospel. Skip ahead a week if you like, but don't feel ashamed or disappointed if you find you've bitten off more than you can chew. Conversely, if you're uncomfortable with a certain week's program, or if you have to miss some workouts because of illness or unavoidable obligations, don't hesitate to stay where you are for another week or so or even to drop back. You will no doubt experience a few aches and pains during the first few weeks as your muscles and joints adjust to the stresses of running. Your legs, hamstrings, and sometimes your abdominal muscles may hurt during those first runs, particularly if you are out of shape. These are nothing to worry about and should go away. Check with your doctor if they don't, however, just to be on the safe side.

I will talk about what causes this pain and how to minimize it in Chapter 7 and discuss more fully the general kinds of pain and injury runners meet up with, their prevention, and their treatment. Then, in Chapter 8, a series of warm-up exercises—stretches and weight lifts that are helpful in preparing for your runs, in preventing injury, and in minimizing pain—is described and illustrated.

New runners may not realize that it is essential to run on an almost empty stomach or else risk discomfort or have to make an unscheduled stop at a restroom or behind the bushes on the road during a run. Optimally, light eating is recommended, which should be done at least an hour and preferably more before a run. The drinking of liquids before and during a long race is a different matter and a necessity. It will be considered in Chapter 5 on 10-kilometer racing and in Chapter 11 on marathoning.

Run easily, and run comfortably. Most important of all, run regularly. For now, those four 30-minute workouts each week are the keys to your running future.

There are some important loose ends to tie up before we move on, one of them being hills.

Hills are the bane of every runner's existence. I said you should avoid them during your first three months—there's no point in spoiling a good thing before you've gotten a fair amount of time under your belt—but this will sometimes be difficult. And as you progress and seek out new courses, it will be downright impossible.

Running hills is 90 percent mental. Most runners fear hills, but after you tackle a few of them, you'll find they're not nearly as bad as everybody said they were and even offer a welcome change of pace. Keep in mind that for every uphill slope there is usually a downhill. This will give you something to look forward to.

There are three points to remember as you run uphill.

• Exaggerate. Exaggerate your arm swing, your knee pump, and your breathing—everything.

• Shorten your stride. The hill will force you to do this automatically, but keep it in mind anyway.

• Maintain your pace. This is the most difficult part of uphill running. You'll huff and puff a lot and think you are perilously close to losing your breath, and near the crest you'll be inclined to reward yourself by slowing down. Don't. You'll have plenty of time to recover on the downhill side.

The trick on the far side of the hill is to let the hill work for you, just as it resisted you on the way up. Lean forward just slightly to let your momentum carry you along, but without overstriding or running too fast. A long, loping stride feels great for a little while, but if you're not careful, you'll soon find yourself out of control and having to brake violently with each step in order to keep from stumbling over yourself. You'll feel those shocks all up and down your legs, and they could take as much out of you as running uphill ever did.

No two runners attack hills in precisely the same way. Ben has bad knees and isn't crazy about running downhill because the constant jolting hurts them tremendously. He compensates by running very strongly uphill. On the other hand, I loaf a little bit running up a hill but make up for my laziness by flying down the other side, right at the edge of control. Hill running is a very individual thing, and it won't take you long to discover which part of it you like the best. Probably you'll just have to accept the fact that going up a hill is hard work and coming down one can be fun—if you relax, stay in control, and don't struggle.

You probably have the choice of working out on any of several running surfaces. Each has its strengths and weaknesses.

The ideal running surface is soft, smooth, and level—an accurate description of a synthetic running track. If there is one available, enjoy it while you can, but don't hesitate to look around for something else when you get bored with running at the same place every day. Running tracks are fine, except for the turns at each end, which put an uneven stress on your legs as you go through them. For a day or a week or even a month, this is of little importance, but get in the habit of regularly reversing directions—running clockwise one day and counterclockwise the next—to balance things out.

Indoor running tracks? They don't particularly turn me on. They are usually eleven to sixteen laps to the mile, often more, and you can get downright dizzy running in the same direction on them for even a mile or two. Most indoor tracks compensate for this, and for the uneven stress on your legs, by pointing runners in a clockwise direction on, say, Monday, Wednesday, and Friday and in a counterclockwise direction on Tuesday, Thursday, and Saturday. Working out on an indoor track is better than not working out at all, but unless there's a tornado or a blizzard going on, there's no reason to use one.

Hard sand, if you have access to an ocean, is a nice change of pace. The only problem is that the beach, of course, slopes toward the water. Like running through turns, this puts an uneven stress on your legs, but you can compensate by simply doing half your run in one direction and half in the other.

I'm not fond of soft sand, however. I recently met a guy who was going to build a sand dune in his backyard—it was a very big backyard—because he remembered that running up and down dunes was a favored training technique of the great Australian running coach Percy Cerutty, whose star pupil, Herb Elliot, once held the world's record for the mile. I didn't discourage him—running up sand dunes will strengthen muscles you didn't even know you had—but I really believe soft sand gives too much and could lead to foot and knee injuries.

Of the three most common surfaces—grass, asphalt, and cement —grass is obviously the softest. It's actually not a bad surface, and I enjoy an occasional run through a park or along the edge of a golf course (being careful not to interfere with play, however. There's no one madder than a golfer who thinks you've contributed to his or her last duck hook). But on balance, grass also loses out. It's often slippery and occasionally too soft, and you always have to be on the lookout for hidden holes, stones, fallen branches, and

other obstacles that can cause a twisted ankle. For this reason, I would never suggest running on grass at night.

That leaves concrete and asphalt. The advantage of concrete is that most sidewalks are made of it, and most sidewalks are level. The disadvantage is that it's about 50 percent harder than asphalt. Although today's running shoes are very well cushioned, I prefer running on asphalt whenever I have the choice.

The disadvantage of asphalt, of course, is that the only place you can find it is on the roadway, where there are also cars and trucks. I can't emphasize enough how important it is for you to be aware of traffic. Every now and again you hear of a runner who's been struck down by a car and either killed or injured. It doesn't happen a lot, but the knowledge that it can ought to be enough of a warning to put you on your guard.

I think Ben and I are more aware of this hazard because we started running in the streets when there weren't too many of us out there. We sometimes had a hard time getting cars to notice us. Today runners are so commonplace that drivers can't help being more aware.

But don't count on it. Dr. Ernst van Aaken, the West German who has done so much to foster the growth of women's marathoning, lost both his legs in 1972 when he was hit by a truck during a workout. While nothing that serious has happened to me or to any of my running friends, there are times when I am sure certain drivers are out to get me. Maybe they're mad at the world or had a bad day at the office—I don't know. But they come flying down the street and barely miss me, even though I am hugging the curb as closely as I can.

Learn to run defensively, just as you were taught to drive a car defensively. Learn to listen for cars around blind curves—you can almost sense them before you see them—and eyeball the drivers until you're sure they're going to pass you by safely. It also doesn't hurt to be thinking of an escape route—a place where you can jump to safety—if a car does swerve out of control. This may seem overly cautious (my friends call me Mother Barron when we're out on the highway because I'm so protective), but it just might save your life.

A final comment on traffic. When Ben and I started running, every time we'd come to a stoplight or a busy intersection and had to wait for traffic we'd continue to jog in place or in strange little circles until the intersection was clear. We felt our training would somehow be diminished if we stopped, if only for a few seconds. Don't worry about interruptions like that. Stop running, and give your legs a little rest until the traffic clears. You're not going to lose anything.

The second problem with roads is that most of them have a slight crown. You will, of course, do most of your road running facing traffic, which means that your left leg will stretch slightly more than your right as you run. Again, over a period of several weeks or even months, this is no problem. But the more you train, the more you should balance this out by running on the right side of the road, even at the risk of having the traffic behind you.

That's about it for now. You can put down this book, if you'd like, and start your own running program. Come back in three months, and we'll see how you've been doing.

5

Trying Something New:
Variety, Speed Work,
and Racing

By now you are running 30 minutes per day, four times a week, and, I hope, feeling pretty good about it. You understand something about technique, you are able to get through your runs without any undue soreness, and you are well on your way to developing a style that is uniquely your own. Perhaps you have even entered an informal race or two—fun runs—just to see what competitive running is all about.

If you are an average runner, you're doing 12 miles per week, knocking off those three 10-minute miles per day with easy regularity. This is no mean feat. (But don't worry if you're doing more or doing less. Distance, remember, is not the true measure of your progress.) More important, you have made your first breakthrough. You have chosen to stick with running and make it a regular and permanent part of your life. You run because you want to run, not because you feel you have to.

Fine, but now it's time to move on. To keep your interest in running strong, to arrive at the point where you may come to even love it, you'll want to vary your runs. This chapter will get you over some more running hurdles. It contains a second schedule, one that is six months long. During this period the number of your

Running with the pack at the L'eggs Race, 1978.

weekly workouts will increase from four to five, and you will be exposed to several more running theories and training methods. Indeed, you will learn just about everything there is to know about running, and should you choose, you will be more than ready to enter and comfortably to run a 10,000-meter race. Unless you are truly interested in marathons or races of even longer distances, you will be capable of setting up your own running schedule, for the rest of your life, really, without any further help from me or anyone else.

This schedule is slightly different from the first one. It is divided into six sections, one for each month. Each section contains that month's running program, explains new training methods I might have added, and offers some general comments and observations about your running as it moves into higher gear.

At the end of the chapter there is a short section on the 10,000-meter race—how to modify your training as one approaches and what to look for while you're running it.

Schedule II

Month One
Run 30 minutes per day, four times per week.

No problem here. The program for this month is exactly the same as the one for the last week of the first schedule. During this month you will firm up the strong running base you've established over the previous thirteen weeks. But as you get used to running steadily and consistently for a set amount of time, you will no doubt also begin to experience that most common of runners' complaints: boredom.

One of the main reasons people stop running is that they lose interest. They work out every day at the same place in the same way with the same people for the same amount of time, and after a while there's just nothing there anymore to keep them coming back. I nearly quit running for this very reason myself. For the first four years of our marriage, Ben and I ran nearly every day at the same high school running track, four laps to the mile, 5 miles per day—twenty laps in all. I reached the point where I cringed even at the thought of our daily run, and I still don't understand how I kept from giving it up.

Then one day Ben and I got to our track, did one lap—and took off through the gate. I don't remember why—probably the track was crowded, and we were feeling claustrophobic—but for sure we were bored and antsy and in need of some variety.

I know this sounds strange today, when most beginning runners just pop out the front door to begin their runs and may never go near a track, but wherever you started, the principle remains the same: vary your workouts as much as you possibly can.

Run different courses. There is no quicker way for tedium to set in than to cover the same territory day after day. All the landmarks become familiar, whether or not you consciously look at them, and soon your easy 30-minute runs seems to drag on forever. In running, anyway, it is really true that familiarity breeds contempt.

How to measure your road courses? The easiest way is to start from your home, run for 15 minutes in one general direction, then turn around and come back. Another is to use your car. By now you should have a pretty good idea how many miles you cover during your 30 minutes. If, for example, you run 3 miles per day, with a little imagination you can map out four or five 3-mile loops that begin and end at your doorstep. By reversing directions on each of them, you create eight to ten different courses for yourself. I've reached the point where I never like to take the same route twice in a row, and with a little bit of work I could probably chart a different course every day of the year. You can, too.

Run with different people. When women complain that running is boring, my first question is do they run alone. Almost invariably the answer is yes. Either they haven't yet gotten their husbands or friends hooked, or they otherwise haven't made the effort to find a running partner. Running with a partner or in a group is much more enjoyable for me than going it alone, and I think it is for most people.

Pick your running partners with some care, however. Find people of approximately your own level. If you are faster than the people you run with, you'll think they're holding you back; if you're slower, you'll want to keep up. Either way, it's bound to be frustrating and ultimately detrimental to your running. Run at your own pace, and follow nobody's schedule but your own.

Vary your speed. On the days you feel spirited and spiffy, step up the pace a little. Not a lot—you still want to run well within yourself and have something left at the end—but just enough so that during your 30 minutes you cover perhaps 3¼ to 3½ miles instead of your normal 3. On those days when you can't really get with it, slow down, even if it means shuffling along for a while or even for the entire length of your workout. Let your body be your guide, without, of course, being lazy.

Play games. If I'm running along a secluded bridle path or on a deserted golf course, I'm not averse to occasionally kicking a soccer ball or tossing a Frisbee back and forth with my partner. Sometimes I'll just count my steps—*one*, two, three, four; *one*, two, three, four—and this seems to help me regain my rhythm on those days when I feel particularly clumsy and awkward.

The best game, though, is mental, and that is the one I mentioned in the previous chapter: concentrating on a particular aspect of your technique. You probably won't want to do this for more than a few minutes at a time, but if you just think about one thing—your arm swing, for example, or your stride length—you'll be surprised not only at how much your running improves but also at how quickly the time passes. Use that checklist often. Pages 73 and 74 ought to be the most-thumbed pages of this book.

Month Two
Run five times per week.
        Day One—40 minutes.
        Day Two—20 minutes.
        Day Three—40 minutes.
        Day Four—20 minutes.
        Day Five—40 minutes.

If all systems are go, you're now ready to step up the pace, and the easiest way is to add a fifth workout to your weekly training schedule.

Notice that you no longer have to run the same number of minutes each day, a fact that should please you immensely. Not only does this add variety to your schedule, but those two short runs spaced between the three 40-minute workouts will seem like a piece of cake. And it's a perfectly valid way to train, too.

The idea of alternating long and short runs is known as the hard-easy principle. I stumbled across it quite by accident years before I learned that it was an accepted training method for distance running.

When I got up to 5 miles per day—back when Ben and I were hooked on distance—a good day's workout would often be followed by a very poor one. It would take me another 3 or 4 minutes to run the same number of miles I'd knocked off so easily the day before. I thought that was it. Ben and I both did. We were convinced that we'd reached some sort of invisible barrier that would be impossible, or at least very painful, for us to cross.

But then on the days when we didn't feel particularly strong, we sometimes started cutting short our planned workouts, and much to our amazement we found that our runs a day or two later were equal in quality to, and sometimes better than, what they had been. What we discovered was that runners go through peaks and valleys. I said earlier that your running will continue to improve simply if you show up, and that's true. But the improvement can't always be measured day to day; rather, you should be content to take a reading once a week, or once a month, or even once every several months to see how you're doing. That's the mistake Ben and I made—thinking we had to do better every time we went out there.

Your body is an amazing instrument, but it isn't indestructible. It's rather like an attacking army, able to advance at a great rate into enemy territory, but then it must pause to regroup—rest its troops and let its supply lines catch up—before the next charge. Every athlete is like this. Ben and I know a weight lifter who works out three times a week and says that on only one of those days can he count on a good session. The other two days are for maintenance.

The same thing is true in running, and that is the basis of the hard-easy theory. You spend one day advancing and the next holding the ground you've won while you build up for the next thrust.

At about the same time that Ben and I incorporated the hard-easy theory into our training, we threw away our stopwatches. I've told you why you don't have to worry about the number of miles you run; now let me explain why you needn't be concerned with how fast you run them. At our old running track, we used to work out with a group of guys who carried stopwatches with them and gave us our splits—our times—after each quarter-mile we ran. Every day. If you don't think that got old. We'd run a great 5 miles one day, and the next time out we'd just feel dead—but those guys would still be there calling out our numbers, every lap.

Worrying about time, I think, is unnecessary for several reasons. By now you should have a pretty good idea of how far you run, and how fast. Let's assume that you're capable of easily running 4 miles during this month's 40-minute runs. Okay. So you start out knowing that you should hit the first milepost right at 10 minutes, the second at 20 minutes, the third at 30 minutes, and the fourth at 40 minutes: boom, boom, boom, boom. But perhaps on one particular day you pick a course with hills on it, or the weather's a little hot, or your body just doesn't feel like going fast. Then you hit the first milepost, check your watch, and find it's taken you 11 minutes, not 10. Your inclination is to speed up, and so you do—with the result that you finish your run drained of energy and with absolutely no enthusiasm for the next day's workout. Either that or you push yourself just enough so that you develop some aches and pains, which eventually turn into tendinitis, inflamed muscles, stress fractures, and the like. Then you're sidelined, perhaps for several weeks, and you've lost a lot of what you've worked so hard to build.

This might seem like an extreme example, but it happens all the time.

Without a stopwatch hanging over your head, your body has the chance to set its own pace, and that is the only voice you ever need pay attention to. You will run with less tension and stress, and over the long haul both the quality and quantity of your running will improve.

(I realize, however, that there are some people who are better off using a stopwatch. Some runners have a lousy sense of pace. Others are plain lazy, and without a stopwatch to guide them they will find improvement difficult. Still others are goal-oriented. They need that stopwatch as much as a racing greyhound needs its mechanical rabbit, or the proverbial donkey its dangling carrot. If you fall into one of these categories, by all means keep that stopwatch with you. But if you find you're getting stale and aren't running as well as you think you should, or if you feel the watch puts too much pressure on you, hide it in a drawer somewhere, and forget about it.)

There is another reason not to concern yourself with distance and speed, and that's because most of us give ourselves too much credit when we lay out our road courses. We use our intuition to judge their lengths and then find out that what we thought was a 4-mile course was really only 3½. I know deep down that my favorite 10-mile course is really only 9¼ miles. Ben once ran a 7-mile course near a friend's home in Michigan and was amazed at his time—until he measured the circuit, accurately, and found it stretched only 6½ miles. But 40 minutes are 40 minutes, and there's no way to shortcut them.

Month Three
Run five times per week.
   Day One—40 minutes.
   Day Two—30 minutes.
   Day Three—40 minutes.
   Day Four—20 minutes.
   Day Five—50 minutes.

What I've added to your schedule this month is a long run. Right now it isn't very long—I've just tacked on 10 minutes to your week's fifth workout—but it will continue to grow, slowly and surely, as we move ahead.

The long run is an integral part of nearly every good distance runner's training schedule and serves two purposes: it measures your overall progress, and it improves the quality of your shorter runs.

It is a sort of chicken-and-egg situation. At first, the long run might seem beyond your capacity. But after you've done a couple of them, your 30- and 40-minute workouts will seem a snap— which in turn will be a sign that you are shoring up your base for the longer run. (I found out the truth of this myself in the twelve months between the 1973 and 1974 Peachtree Road Races. I won both of them, and my time the second year was 2 minutes, 7 seconds faster than the first, although the only change in my training schedule was the addition of a single long run each week.) Don't push yourself too much during your long run. Run well within yourself, so that at the end of it you feel pleasantly tired but not fatigued.

This month is perhaps the most critical of the schedule. You are running 3 hours per week, and your total mileage is right around 20 per week, give or take a mile. (Let's assume that you can now easily run a mile in 9 minutes.) This seems to be the level at which a runner's body begins to rebel. Minor aches and pains that used to go away on their own now stick around longer. Despite every precaution, you might experience sore muscles, inflamed tendons, and generally creaky joints. You are running longer and faster, but you are also beginning to pay the price. It's time to make another breakthrough and find a way to get past this barrier without unduly punishing your body.

The way to do this is by not overtraining, which is the second major problem that runners face (the first, remember, was boredom) and can be easily defined as doing too much too fast too soon. And the easiest way to avoid overtraining is to listen to your body—before, during, and after your workouts.

Let me explain how this works.

Your body has several built-in monitors, the most important and easily accessible of which is your pulse rate. Get in the habit of taking your pulse when you wake up in the morning, immediately at the end of a workout, and then about 4 minutes after your run is finished. (There are two easy ways to measure your pulse: at your wrist or by placing your thumb and forefinger on either side of your Adam's apple until you feel the surge of blood in your carotid artery. Count the beats for 10 seconds and multiply by 6, or for 15 seconds and multiply by 4.) My resting pulse rate is 40, at the end of a run it's about 150, and 4 minutes later drops to between 90 and 100. (Don't be alarmed if your numbers are different from mine. Everybody's heart beats to a different drummer.) If, for example, I wake up and my pulse rate is 55 or 60, I'm pretty sure that I've done too much, and I would seriously consider running very easily this particular day, or not at all. If at the end of a run my recovery time is slower than usual—if my pulse rate is 120 after 4 minutes—I'm likewise reasonably certain that I've overextended myself.

Similarly, your sleeping habits are an excellent clue to your general well-being. Most people find that after a few months of running they sleep very well—very long and very deeply. If I am tired but still can't get to sleep or if my sleep is erratic and restless, I also consider this a warning.

Finally, your general aches and pains are a good health guide. I've never been particularly fond of pain myself, but once you get up to where you're running 3 hours per week—which you now are —a certain soreness is inevitable. This isn't any problem and will usually go away after a few minutes of easy jogging. But pain is a warning from your body that says, "Hold it, you're hurting me," and if the soreness persists or even if you've just got the blahs, it's usually a solid sign that you're drained.

So. Start evaluating yourself right from the moment you wake up, and keep on taking readings until you step out the door for your run. Most days there won't be any problem, but perhaps once a week, or once every two weeks, your body will signal that all is not well and that you should tone down your workout or cancel it entirely.

Sometimes you won't be able to decide until after you're well into your run. The primary clue is whether or not you get your second wind. As I said before, you'll always huff and puff through the first six or seven minutes of a workout before you break out into a nice sweat and your breathing becomes relaxed. But when this doesn't happen, watch out. Dr. George Sheehan, the author of *Running and Being* and several other excellent running books, says that if he doesn't get his second wind on schedule, he stops right there, turns around, and goes home. I wouldn't go quite that far, but I would slow down to the laziest jog possible or maybe even walk for a few minutes. Then give it another shot. If your second wind still doesn't show, call it a day. You won't lose a thing.

But even if you do get your second wind on time, you still might not feel all that great as you move into high gear. If this happens, don't hesitate to cut back—again, even to the point of going home. This is common advice that nearly every running authority offers, but it is also perhaps the most ignored. You've gone to the trouble to change into your running gear, you're out there, and you feel guilty about quitting. Don't—feel guilty, that is. If you continue running, you'll do yourself more harm than good.

There are two general points to be made about all this. The first is: don't lock yourself into a schedule. Decide how long you're going to run on the basis of what your body tells you, not what's written down on a piece of paper. If you use a schedule as gospel, you might end up running 20 minutes, or even resting, on a good day when you're capable of knocking off that 50-minute long run, or you might absolutely punish yourself to the point of injury by doing the long run on a day when you ought to be lounging by the pool.

Use your off days judiciously. For starters, I would recommend resting the day after your long run and the day after your second 40-minute run—Day Three. But if you need two days to recover from the long run, take them. Don't feel you have to push. You're in competition with absolutely nobody except yourself.

The second point is never to leave your workout on the track. Several years ago Ben and I started noticing a runner—a really fine runner—who always walked a mile after his workouts, no matter if he'd been jogging for 20 minutes or pushing hard for 2 hours. "I always want to feel good when I stop," he told us, "because if I don't, I'm not coming back tomorrow. And I want to come back."

In a poetic book called *The Zen of Running*, author Fred Rohé says this in another way: "Always do less than you think you can."

One way is to slow down during the last few minutes of your workout. If you've planned to run 40 minutes, jog, or even walk, the last 5. You'll return home refreshed and eager for the next day's training.

Another way is to run more slowly than you think you can, which, if you have been paying attention, you already are. I have urged you to stay under control, to run within your limits, to use the Talk Test, and to listen to your body. All these are ways of explaining a principle known as long, slow distance training—LSD for short—a phrase coined several years ago by Joe Henderson, a columnist for *Runner's World*. It says the same thing: less is best. By running more slowly than you think you can over longer distances, you develop the physiological systems you want to develop with a minimum of pain and a maximum of enjoyment.

My favorite overtraining story concerns Wayne Robinson, one of several Atlanta runners who trained heavily for the 1978 Boston

Marathon, ran it well (he was one of the celebrants at what turned out to be my victory party), then crashed and laid off for several weeks. He came back, but for months he never ran more than 4 or 5 miles per day, and well within his limits. "And y'know," he said, "it was so much more fun. I wasn't on a schedule, I didn't have to burn it on certain days, and I could just go out and take it easy. I really got to love running again."

Which is the whole point. Take time to stop and smell the roses.

Month Four
Run five times per week.
> Day One—40 minutes.
> Day Two—30 minutes.
> Day Three—40 minutes, Fartlek.
> Day Four—30 minutes.
> Day Five—60 minutes.

Until now I have been talking mainly about the quantity of your workouts and very little about their quality. Now it is time to think about how fast you run as well as how far and for how long.

For the three months of your beginners' schedule and for the first three months of this one, you have been running aerobically —that is, during your long, slow runs you have used up less oxygen than you have taken in. Since distance running is fundamentally an aerobic exercise, for years the prevailing attitude among distance runners was that if you wanted to run long distances, the best way to train for them was to run long distances. To a degree, of course, that was true. But in time runners realized that this wasn't the whole story, that if they added a different kind of workout to their schedule, one that emphasized speed rather than distance, their times would improve dramatically. Thus was speed training born.

Speed work is anaerobic—you use up *more* oxygen than you take in—and it serves several purposes. It offers a nice change of pace from your regular training. It stretches your muscles. It forces your cardiovascular system into high gear and also teaches your body to draw upon other sources of energy when it is in a state of oxygen debt. In short, if long, slow distance training builds your bodily engine, speed work provides it with a very effective after-burner.

There are several kinds of speed training. One of the most popular is Fartlek, devised in the 1930s by a Swedish track coach by the name of Gösta Holmer. Literally translated, Fartlek means "speed play," and that's precisely what it is. You run at your normal, slow pace, and when the mood strikes you, you sprint for a short distance. Then you return to your regular pace. Actually, *sprint* is the wrong word, for it implies flat-out running, and that's not really what you do. You "stride," at a speed approximately halfway between normal and flat out. Fartlek allows you all sorts of freedom—that's the joy of it—but until you figure out your own routine, let me suggest ten to twelve strides during your 40-minute workout, each one between 100 yards and 880 yards. Just pick out a telephone pole, a house, or some other convenient landmark down the road, stride to it; then jog along until you feel ready to burn it again.

Fartlek is a good, solid workout, but the same principle applies to it as to your regular runs. Don't overdo it. When you finish, you shouldn't be worn out. This can be your most enjoyable training day of the week. Make sure that it is.

Month Five
Run five times per week.

   Day One—45 minutes.
   Day Two—30 minutes.
   Day Three—45 minutes of Fartlek or intervals.
   Day Four—30 minutes.
   Day Five—70 minutes.

The most common kind of speed work is interval training. Like Fartlek, the idea is to alternate strides with recovery jogs to increase your body's ability to perform in a state of oxygen debt. Unlike Fartlek, interval training is formal and precise, and for this reason you should do it at a running track whenever possible. A running track is usually 440 yards around, and the distances of the intervals are easily measured.

There are a hundred different kinds of interval workouts. Here are four of them.

INTERVAL A—Run the straightaways of your running track and jog the curves. Keep doing this for a total of eight laps.

INTERVAL B—Run 220 yards and jog 220 yards. Repeat for a total of eight laps.

INTERVAL C—Run 110 yards, jog 110 yards; run 220 yards, jog 110 yards; run 330 yards, jog 110 yards; run 440 yards, jog 110 yards. Do this entire sequence once more, from the top.

INTERVAL D—Run 110 yards, jog 110 yards; run 220 yards, jog 110 yards; run 330 yards, jog 110 yards; run 440 yards, jog 440 yards; run 440 yards, jog 110 yards; run 330 yards, jog 110 yards; run 220 yards, jog 110 yards; run 110 yards, jog 110 yards.

Do your interval training almost the same way as you would Fartlek. Run each interval at a speed about halfway between your normal pace and flat-out, and jog slowly in between—just shuffle along so you're almost walking. The purpose of the recovery jogs is to let you get back most—but not all—of your wind, and replace most—but not all—of the oxygen you used up during your strides. If you're not recovering sufficiently—your pulse should drop to around 110, although this will vary from runner to runner—keep on jogging until you do.

The four intervals I've shown are listed in order of their intensity, and this is how I suggest you plug them into your running schedule. This month, do Fartlek the first week, Interval A the second, Fartlek the third, and Interval B the fourth.

Next month—Month Six—begin with Interval C the first week, continue with Interval D the second, Interval B the third, and Interval C the fourth.

I haven't yet mentioned hill workouts because you might be hard pressed to find some good slopes near your home. If there are, however, don't hesitate to substitute time on the hills for your weekly Fartlek or interval workout. Run hard for 100 yards or so uphill, and slowly jog down, and repeat eight to ten times. This is an excellent drill, and I guarantee that if you do it a couple of times, interval training—and certainly Fartlek—will be a snap. (In the absence of hills, run the steps at a football stadium or in the stairwell of your office building. The results will be the same.) Obviously, this won't take 40 or 45 minutes. Fill the time by running normally both before and after your hill workout.

Indeed, precede all your speed workouts, whether Fartlek, intervals, or hills, with a solid warm-up run of at least 6 to 7 minutes, just enough to let you taste your second wind. Similarly, take an equal amount of time to shuffle around and cool down at the end of them. Don't leave your workouts at the track or on the road, and especially don't leave them in the hills.

Month Six
Run five days per week.

        Day One—45 minutes.
        Day Two—30 minutes.
        Day Three—45 minutes of intervals.
        Day Four—30 minutes.
        Day Five—80 minutes.

I've added nothing new to your schedule for this month. Indeed, there's nothing more to add. All of running's basic tools are at your disposal, and anything else you learn will be a refinement of fundamental principles.

You understand that the different kinds of workouts I've described—the long run, the short runs mixed in with long runs, and speed training (Fartlek or intervals)—are all proven ways to increase your capacity and tolerance for running and are designed to help you run as far and as fast as your temperament and genes will allow.

You understand that running involves repetition—lots of it—but that it doesn't have to be boring or tedious. The number of different workouts and their different lengths, plus the variety of courses over which they can be done, mean that you rarely have to do precisely the same kind of training twice.

You understand the danger of overtraining. By not being competitive, by always running well within your limits, and by not hesitating to cut short or even cancel a workout entirely, you can avoid hurting yourself or becoming washed out.

What you do next with your running is entirely up to you. Nine months ago, you were walking 20 minutes per day; now you are running 3 hours, 45 minutes per week. During the past six months alone, your mileage has jumped from around 12 per week to almost 30 (although you know that distance is not an important yardstick of your progress).

Like my first schedule, this training program is meant to be a guideline. If it suits you, fine. Stick with it. But if it doesn't, don't hesitate to fiddle with it until it does. If you feel you're being asked to do too much, shorten your long run by a few minutes, do the easier intervals, modify them, or cut them out entirely and stick with Fartlek on your speed days—or drop back a month. If you still feel stale, rest for three or four days—even longer—and see if that doesn't restore your pep and enthusiasm. If, on the other hand, you feel my pace is too slow, be patient. Chapter 11 outlines a third training program that could have you running your first marathon in another nine months.

Be flexible in your training. What Ben and I do—and you have been running long enough to consider this yourself—is figure out very roughly what kind of training we want to do each week. We know we want to do a long run and one day of speed work, but the rest of the time we run only according to how we feel. If we run 15 minutes more than we planned on a given day, we chop off some time somewhere else. If we cut short a workout, we add on the lost minutes wherever we conveniently can. By approaching your training this way, you'll put in the required number of minutes over a given period of time, but each workout will be only as long as your body says it should be. And that is the bottom line.

Okay, let's go racing. Any race at any moderate distance will do, but 10,000-meter runs (6.2 miles) seem to be the most popular event nowadays, and you are more than ready for that. Besides, a race, and the preparation for it, will offer a nice break from your regular training.

In the last week before the race, cut your workouts by about 50 percent. Runners who have never raced tend to come to their first starting line very much overtrained. Pooped out, in fact. But after nine months of steady running, you have built a very solid base. By cooling it the last week, you'll acquire a good reserve of energy by the time the starter's gun goes off.

Let's assume the race is scheduled for a Saturday (as, in fact, most of them are), and back up seven days.

Sunday—Take the day off.

Monday—Run 30 minutes easily. Don't loaf, but don't burn it either. If you've been training at an 8-minute-per-mile pace, do this workout at a 9-minute pace, nothing faster.

Tuesday—Same thing.

Wednesday—Get in some speed work, but nothing serious. Start with a 10-minute warm-up run, then do eight 220-yard strides with 220-yard recovery jogs in between. This is my Interval B, but don't run it as fast as you normally would. Make it an easy workout, with no real huffing and puffing.

Thursday—Take the day off.

Friday—Jog 15 or 20 minutes, just to warm up gently. Some runners like to take both Thursday and Friday off before a weekend race, but I find I lose my feeling for running if I miss two days in a row. This little run the day before keeps you in touch.

Regarding your diet, my advice is simple: Don't change anything. First of all, you should experiment with your diet during your regular training rather than immediately before a race, just in case your body reacts badly to any new foodstuffs you might be tempted to offer it. Second, a special runners' diet—such as the carbohydrate loading in vogue among marathoners—will have little effect in a race of this distance. The night before, however, you could avoid red meat and concentrate on complex carbohydrates such as fruits, vegetables, and brown rice and other whole grains. Also, drink two or three extra glasses of water or fruit juice.

Similarly, the day of the race, eat gently. Most races are held in the morning, and since it takes between three and four hours to digest a substantial amount of food, either you will have to eat breakfast very early, or you will be forced to run on a full stomach, neither of which is desirable. Instead, have some toast and fruit juice a couple of hours before the race, and again, force yourself to drink a couple of extra glasses of fruit juice or water, particularly if the day promises to be on the warm side. I also like a cup or two of coffee, although I suspect the race-day benefits of caffeine are mostly psychological.

Try to sleep well the night before the race, but don't be terribly upset if you can't. Nerves and tension might make that impossible. (One night before a 1975 marathon in New York City, neither Ben nor I got any sleep at all. We were staying in a very old and creaky hotel, the beds were terrible, and our room was right next to an air shaft. It didn't make any difference—to me. I finished third in a time of 2 hours, 58 minutes on a very hot day. Ben, however, dropped out.) Instead, concentrate on getting a full night's rest *two* nights before the race. Then you're covered.

Get to the racecourse at least an hour before the gun. This gives you plenty of time to park your car (don't laugh—there's nothing more maddening than to arrive at a race late and find the only parking lot is a mile from the start), check in with the race officials, get your number, and start thinking about the race. You don't want any last-minute surprises, and this extra hour will give you plenty of time to deal with any.

About 20 minutes before the start, begin warming up. At all the 10,000-meter races I've ever entered, a majority of the contestants just stand around before the start or perhaps do some moderate stretching. But I'll always see around fifty runners doing very extensive warm-ups, and they are the ones who invariably nail down the first fifty places.

Run a good, solid mile. Do the first third at a moderate jog, the second third a little faster, and the final third at very close to your racing pace. This may seem like a lot, but at the end you should just be breaking into your second wind. Which is precisely what you want. It's not fair to ask your body to go racing without some advance warning. Now do some good stretches, and head for the starting line 3 or 4 minutes before the gun. (This, of course, assumes the race starts on time. If it doesn't, jog around and keep loose until it does begin.)

Don't go to the starting line without a plan. Project a realistic finishing time for yourself, and be conservative. Then figure out what your times should be at the 1-mile mark and the 3-mile mark. These are your key splits.

Know the course. Several days before the race, go over the entire 10,000 meters carefully—in a car or on a bike, if you don't want to run it—noting particularly the location of any hills as well as the landmarks at those 1- and 3-mile marks. On the day of the race, be aware of other conditions that could affect your time, such as excessive heat or humidity or a strong wind.

At most 10,000-meter races, the runners line up for the start more or less according to their ability, with the fastest runners at the front. Often there will be signs posted—6-minute milers near the front, followed by 7-minute milers, followed by 8-minute

The start of the L'eggs 10-Kilometer Race in New York City, 1979.

milers, and so on. If you're unsure where to go, ask a race official when you arrive at the course.

There will no doubt be bedlam when the gun goes off—there always is. Your goal is to run the entire race at an even pace. If, for example, you are an 8-minute miler, you will have projected your finishing time at 50 minutes. This means you should hit the mile markers precisely every 8 minutes.

The first mile of the race is the most difficult. The enthusiasm of the pack causes nearly everybody in it to go out too fast—that plus the fear of getting trampled by the runners behind you. Try as best you can to maintain the pace you've set for yourself, and remember that it's much more difficult to go out too fast and have to hang on than it is to start slowly and pick up the pace near the end.

Splits are given in different ways at different races. At some, race officials shout them out every mile; at others only at the 1- and 3-mile marks. A few races let the runners figure out for themselves how fast they're going.

Even if the splits are to be called out, don't count on being able to hear them. Know your 1-mile landmark, and when you reach it, check your watch, or, if you aren't carrying one, ask around. Some other nearby runner is bound to have one. If you've started too fast, slow down. And of course, if you're behind your pace at the end of the first mile, pick it up a little.

Between the first and third miles take a good reading of yourself. Are you breathing easily? Are you relaxed? Is your arm swing good? In general, run down the checklist on pages 73 and 74, and also start listening to your body.

If you reach the halfway point (the 3-mile marker) on schedule, the rest of the race will take care of itself. If you're ahead of schedule, seriously consider slowing down. If you're behind schedule, figure out why. If it's because you don't feel great, slow down even more. This is your first race, and there will be many others. If it's because you've been mentally lazy, start concentrating again until you get back into it.

Ben and I coming in to finish the Peachtree Road Race in Atlanta, 1973.

At no time during this race, particularly since it's your first, should you concern yourself with any other runner. This is your race alone, and your only goal is to keep to that conservative schedule you set for yourself.

That is not to say you can't use other runners. If, for example, you're struggling on a hill, it's quite acceptable to latch onto another runner and let him or her pace you to the top. Or if you're unsure of your own pace generally, key onto a runner who seems to be moving at a comfortable speed. But be careful not to be lured into running at another competitor's pace.

Don't be tempted to pick up the pace too much, even if you're feeling good, until the finish line is practically in sight. More than anything, you want this race to be a good experience for you, and there's nothing more disheartening than to slog across your first finish line out of breath and feeling miserable.

Finishes, like starts, are handled in a variety of ways. Usually an official will hand you a finishing number as you cross the line, but if there are several hundred runners, you may be temporarily channeled into a chute of some sort until the officials can catch up with their work.

After you have been processed at the finish, get yourself a drink, and then jog an easy half-mile, just to release the tensions of the race and protect yourself against stiffness. And if you're up to it, do a few postrace stretches.

Then take the next day off. Congratulations.

Marty Cooksey wins the
Avon Marathon in Cincinnati, 1979.

Craig Virgin in a moment of triumph at the
Falmouth (Mass.) 7.2-Mile Road Race, 1979

6

Stress and
the Mind-Body System

The human organism is a precise orchestration of several different physiological systems and mental processes that are inseparable and that together compose what practitioners of holistic healing call the bodymind or the mind-body system. The body is a structure made up of several subsystems—such as the pulmonary and cardiovascular systems (the lungs, heart, and blood vessels), the musculoskeletal system, the digestive system and the urinary system, the endocrine system—the workings of which are controlled by the central nervous systems. The mind produces thought, which is defined as reason, and emotion, or strong feeling. While it is possible to identify thought, feeling, and the various physical subsystems and for convenience's sake discuss them in isolation from the whole, they are, in fact, interdependent. It is impossible for something to happen in one part of the bodymind without its affecting the whole.

Acting at all times on the mind-body system is stress, which is any physical, chemical, thermal, or psychological change inside or outside the body strong enough to cause the system to react. Intelligence is that which reacts to stress by always trying to restore balance. If the stress is sufficiently great to override the intelligence working to adapt to it, tension results. But if the intelligence is able to deal with stress and keep the system in balance, then improvement in health is possible.

Quite often either the mind-body system is in balance or the stresses working on it are normal, positive stresses—such as a gentle breeze, a warm bath, a good conversation, the presence of a loved one—and are of no concern. Our intelligence is in control, and we feel good.

But let's say it's Friday afternoon, and you're cleaning off your desk after a hard week's work in anticipation of a long weekend in the mountains with your family. Just before you're about to leave, the boss walks in, presents you with a stack of files, and says he or she needs a report on them first thing Monday morning. What happens to you?

Your first response is emotional—anger. Your second is a thoughtful *How can I weasel my way out of this?* At the same time, various chemical reactions take place that result in certain glands secreting certain hormones that in short order give you an upset stomach. Finally, as you belligerently burn the midnight oil all weekend, having come up with no way out, you find yourself with a painfully stiff neck and a gruesome headache. And you come down with a cold. Stress has won out over intelligence and produced tension, the symptoms of which you are now experiencing.

Or let's say you're invited to a dinner party. The company is superb, and so are the food and the wine. There are seconds all around, and of course, who can resist the chocolate mousse and the after-dinner drinks? You return home with a grin on your face, feeling great. The next morning, however, your stomach is upset, you've got a headache, and you're weak in the knees. You're also in an absolutely foul mood, put out with the world, almost depressed, and you can't concentrate long enough to get through the lead story in the morning newspaper. You are, in short, hung over. Once again, stress has won out over intelligence.

Although in the first case the cause of your stress was largely mental—having to work when you wanted to play—and in the second it was mainly physical—eating and drinking too much—the results were very much the same. And so it is with every instance of excessive stress, an important point to keep in mind.

Running affects the mind-body system because it is a form of stress. Up to a point it is a positive stress of the kind the bodymind intelligence can easily deal with to keep the system in balance. Beyond a certain point, however, running overwhelms the system's intelligence and produces mental anguish or physical pain and usually both. This point—let's call it the exhaustion point, or the collapse point, or, better yet, the teeter point—is hard to keep track of and changes constantly. The truth of this is that you can sometimes breeze through a 60-minute run on Tuesday and finish eager for more, but on Thursday a 30-minute "easy-day" run becomes a literal pain. As I've said in other ways, your ability to recognize this point and react intelligently when you approach it is one of the keys—perhaps the major key—to having a successful and enjoyable running career.

An additional difficulty is that factors that appear to be totally unrelated to running may be at work to lower your collapse point. A case in point is me. By the middle of 1979 I had had a bad hamstring pull for nearly two years. At the same time I entered an intensely upsetting period in my personal life. I started to think about giving up competitive running. Although I am forever preaching against running through pain, I did, unable to resolve the conflict. As I guess is my nature, I experimented with everything and everybody I could think of. Nothing and nobody worked.

Then quite by chance I met Dr. Stan Dawson, a chiropractor who directs a holistic health care center here in Atlanta. He listened to me and suggested I was like a car whose driver had one foot on the brake and the other on the accelerator. A part of me was eager to push ahead, but the rest was just as eager to draw back a little. The tension, which I thought was mainly mental, really had its roots in the fact of my pulled hamstring and my unwillingness to ease up in my training long enough to let it heal. Once Dr. Dawson explained this to me, I was able to make some fundamental decisions. I reduced my training and submitted to therapy. Shortly after that my tension, which had also manifested itself physically in an awesome collection of very tight muscles, began to go away. I soon got my entire mind-body system back in balance, and within two months I was able to turn in some of the best interval times of my life. I felt better about my running than I had in two years.

The body works in roughly the following way:
In order to stay alive, the body needs food, of which there are

three kinds. Carbohydrates break down to form glucose, which is the body's source of fuel and is stored in the muscles and liver as glycogen. Fat is required for insulation and also serves as an emergency fuel store. (The body can maintain only a certain quantity of carbohydrates. Any excess is immediately converted to fat. Unfortunately the body can maintain a practically unlimited amount of fat.) Protein is necessary to build new cells and repair damaged ones. The body also needs water to flush out waste, and vitamins and minerals to help regulate and control the essential and ongoing chemical reactions known as cellular metabolism. Finally, oxygen is necessary for life because without it the body could not burn—oxidize—its fuel.

Blood is the body's internal transportation system, and the heart is the transportation system's pump. Blood picks up oxygen from the lungs and stored glycogen from the liver—after it has been converted to glucose—and delivers both, on demand from the brain, to parts of the body that request them. At the same time the blood picks up waste from the cells. The blood then passes through the kidneys, which filter the waste from it (which waste leaves the body in the urine), and the lungs, which remove carbon dioxide, an unwanted by-product resulting from the burning of glucose and oxygen.

All these systems are regulated by the endocrine system and the nervous system.

There are other ways to describe how the body works, but the beauty of the bodymind concept is that all the physical systems and mental processes are connected and interdependent, so it is possible to enter the circle at any point and from there describe the workings of the whole. Because the cardiovascular system is the one that receives the greatest stress—and the greatest benefit—from running, let's continue from there.

Since running is a stress, this means there must be responses to it. These responses take place in four stages, whether you jog an easy 3 miles or run a hard marathon. Let's look at those responses and examine the relationship of running to the workings of the mind-body system.

The preparation.   Even before you begin to run, the nervous system and the endocrine system are preparing your body for exercise.

THE HEART-LUNG MACHINE

Oxygenated blood is pumped from the left side of the heart (by the left ventricle) to the aorta. Via a series of branch arteries and even smaller capillaries, this fresh blood is distributed to all parts of the body. It carries oxygen, hormones, nutrients, and other substances to the tissues that need them, and at the same time it removes from the tissues carbon dioxide and other waste products. After the blood is filtered by the kidneys, it flows to the right side of the heart, which pumps it to the lungs. In the lungs, carbon dioxide is removed from the blood and oxygen is added to it. Finally, the blood returns to the left side of the heart—and the circulatory process begins anew.

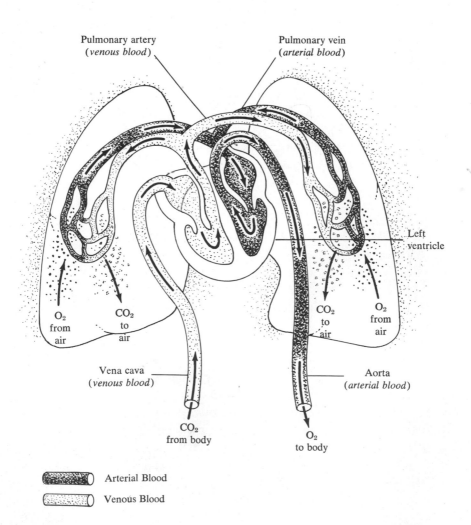

The nervous system is the quick-acting connecting link between your mind and your body. When you make the decision to run, your nervous system transmits this information to your body—and your body also transmits information to your mind, telling you what kind of physical shape you're in.

At the same time the slower-acting endocrine system, a network of glands, goes to work. These glands secrete chemical messengers —called hormones—directly into the bloodstream and in concert with the nervous system regulate all the activities of the body's organs and tissues. One gland in particular, the pancreas, secretes a hormone that instructs the blood to begin extracting stored glycogen, in the form of glucose, from the liver. This raises the blood-sugar level of the body and further prepares it for exercise. At the same time the adrenal gland secretes a hormone that stimulates the heart.

An interesting and important aspect of this preparation, which takes place even as you're changing into your shorts, shoes, and singlet, is that these two systems know whether or not you are a regular runner. If you run on a schedule—at five o'clock every afternoon, for example—they begin to prepare for exercise even before you make the conscious decision to run. If you run infrequently, they are caught by surprise and work at less than full strength. If you run erratically, they are simply confused. It seems regularity is a very important factor in training the mind and the body.

The start. When you actually set out down the road, your body undergoes rapid changes in cardiovascular physiology. Your heart rate and blood flow increase, and your blood pressure goes up. Arteries, which carry oxygen and glucose to the nether parts of your body, begin to dilate, particularly those in the muscles most directly affected by running. At the same time veins, which carry waste-laden blood back toward the heart (via the kidneys and lungs), are squeezed by contractions of the abdominal wall, thus increasing the return flow. Since your body has a finite quantity of blood, the overall effect of these sudden and dramatic changes is to draw blood away from the internal organs, most significantly, for our demonstration purposes, the kidneys and those of the gastrointestinal system.

The sudden change in physiology explains the need for a good warm-up before you run or at least the desirability of starting out slowly. If you head out the door at full force, your nervous system and endocrine system don't have enough time to warn the rest of your system of what is about to take place. Your muscles, for example, literally won't get warmed up fast enough, and this is when you can pull and otherwise injure them. It's like taking your car from zero to 60 mph in 8 seconds rather than in 15 or 20.

The adjustment. After you've been out on the road for 6 or 7 minutes, your system, having gotten through the shock of the start of the run, begins to fine-tune itself in an effort to bring your entire system back into balance—or at least to accommodate the stress as best it can.

You get your second wind. This is the signal that the diversion of blood away from your internal organs to your muscles—and perhaps your skin—is complete and that your heart and lungs have gotten cranked up and are operating at nearly their full capacity.

This is also the beginning of the deep training part of your run, when certain parts of the mind-body system learn to increase their capacities and stretch their limits. Your body's basic metabolism acquires a new focus. It is now geared up to provide energy for those parts of your body that need it the most. At the same time your body is learning how to provide the extra glucose and oxygen necessary to create that energy.

Let's begin with the heart, where an amazing transformation is taking place. When you first take up running, your untrained heart gets tired much more quickly than your muscles, an important fact of which you are not really aware. Your lungs are doing just fine, the muscles in your legs feel okay, you don't get any distress signals from your internal organs, but your heart is pooped—it, too, needs fresh blood. Most definitely it is under stress. And how does the system intelligently react to provide itself with more blood? In the short run, the heart simply beats faster. But your system goes one step further. It constructs for the heart additional blood vessels and capillaries so that the heart can take on and utilize blood more rapidly. This is called collateral circulation.

This doesn't happen overnight, but over the course of several weeks and months your heart becomes stronger. It learns to pump blood rapidly and efficiently, and since it retains this ability when you're not running, your resting heart rate drops dramatically, from 70 or perhaps even 80 beats per minute to 60 or 50 or even less. (Mine dropped from 78 beats per minute in my prerunning years to around 40, where it is now.) For the same reason, your heart rate returns to normal more quickly after a workout, and during a run its peak rate will slowly lessen as the months go by. And this, in a sentence, is why running—and every other kind of aerobic exercise—is good for you. A trained heart can carry a bigger work load, and more easily, than an untrained heart.

In a similar fashion, your lungs also become more efficient, able to supply the demanding bloodstream with more oxygen more quickly, and extract greater amounts of carbon dioxide.

Cardiovascular stress is also experienced in the muscles of the legs. At rest, the system is in balance, and the bloodstream is easily able to furnish these muscles with their metabolic supplies and take away the waste. When you run, however, the muscles need more glucose and a more efficient disposal system. Again, collateral circulation is the answer. Additional blood vessels are built and, like those already in place, dilate rapidly to accommodate the stress. If you run too long, however, the waste materials cannot be carried away fast enough. The result is a breakdown of muscle cells, which causes pain. One of these metabolic waste products is lactic acid, and it is thought (although not known for sure) that this is the source of muscle soreness the morning after a run. So many cells have broken down that the blood has not yet been able to repair the damage and cart away the debris. This is when your nervous system sends impulses to the brain suggesting that it would be best if you took the day off or at least cut short your workout. Listen to these suggestions, and weigh them carefully. They'll tell you a lot.

The body of the trained runner prepares for exercise, as I've said, by quickly and efficiently converting glycogen, stored in the blood and muscles, into glucose. Glucose is first obtained from carbohydrates and then from the breakdown of fat. There are two kinds of fat. Stored fat is the kind that is usually found where you don't want it to be, on the hips, buttocks, and thighs. An average woman is 23 percent stored fat. With training, she can reduce this to perhaps 17 percent, sometimes less. (An average man is about

17 percent stored fat. He can reduce his percentage to under 10, and in rare cases to less than 5.) But muscle also contains fat. This is desirable fat, however, for it holds the muscle's reserve store of glucose, and in a trained runner the percentage of muscle fat is significantly higher than that in a nonrunner. Again, this is another example of the mind-body system's acting to bring itself into balance in the face of stress and even anticipating the stress.

The challenge. Now you are well into your workout. Your system has readjusted itself, and everything feels great. What happens next depends on several factors, such as how hard you are running and how far, how long you've been a runner, the outside temperature, what you ate for breakfast, and your mental well-being, to name just a few—in short, the factors that are constantly contriving to define your limits. These limits, as I've indicated, can be expanded through training, but they cannot be eliminated. If they are exceeded, tension results. Then the mind-body system swings into action to neutralize this excess stress. Usually the results are rather innocuous, but sometimes they can be quite dramatic.

A small example:

The digestive process, like everything else, depends on a large and healthy blood supply. During exercise, however, the blood flow is diverted from the gastrointestinal organs, including the stomach and the upper intestine, and digestion slows down and sometimes stops entirely. If there is little in your stomach in need of digestion, there's no problem. But if you've gulped down a hearty breakfast just before your run, it will just sit in your stomach, fermenting or putrefying. This is why you shouldn't run after a heavy meal and why you should eat food that is easily and quickly digested.

A larger example:

When stress becomes extreme, it threatens to put an intolerable burden on your kidneys, your muscles, your ability to get rid of excess heat, and your powers of reasoning.

As you approach your limit, certain things begin to happen. Your body heats up two to four degrees above normal. Your body gets rid of excess heat in several ways, but all of them depend on the ability of your cardiovascular system to bring blood to the surface of your skin, where it is then cooled by the outside air. Therefore, there is maximum blood flow to your skin. At the same time there is also maximum blood flow to your muscles and minimum flow to your internal organs, including the kidneys. Finally, there is an accumulation of waste in your muscle cells, which your blood is carrying off to your kidneys. The situation is critical: you are near your teeter point. What happens next is entirely up to you because at this point you are feeling acute discomfort in a lot of areas.

You are thinking, *Slow down.* Your emotions, however, are telling you that you've got only another 15 or 20 minutes to go and why not gut it out.

You decide to push on. In the worst of scenarios, any one of several things could happen, none of them good. Your kidneys, deprived of blood and unable to dispose of the waste they have filtered from the blood, slow down and could perhaps fail entirely. If this doesn't happen, there will still be an awesome dispute between your muscles and your skin over your finite blood supply. If your skin wins out, the buildup of waste in your muscles will cause them to cramp or go into spasms. If the muscles win out, you will become overheated and suffer heat prostration or heat stroke, in which case you could well pass out. Either result is the body's way of effectively and intelligently getting you, the mind-body system, to stop and relieve the excess tension. And your nervous system, having had to mediate this struggle, is probably a shambles, too.

Admittedly, this is an extreme description of what could happen when you run. There's no cause for concern if you run moderately. It does explain, however, why the three great problems for marathoners are kidney failure, muscle spasm, and heat stroke.

A less obvious kind of running stress, of special interest to women, again involves the endocrine system, particularly the ovaries.

In 1978 I participated in a study by three Atlanta doctors and a registered nurse designed to draw a physical fitness profile of the female runner and also to study her reproductive physiology. Forty-eight women between the ages of eighteen and forty-three were selected from one of four categories: marathoners, distance runners (these were women who hadn't run the marathon but had trained as much as 18 miles at a time and were considered capable of it), athletic controls (women who engaged in regular physical activity other than running), and sedentary controls. The results were somewhat predictable, but interesting nonetheless. (A report of this study appeared in the January 1979 issue of *The Physician and Sportsmedicine.*) Here are some of the areas in which the runners differed significantly from the two control groups:

	Marathoners	Distance Runners	Athletic Controls	Sedentary Controls
Weight (pounds)	117.3	110.9	127.5	129.7
Body fat (percent)	18.09	18.39	19.88	21.88
Resting heart rate (supine)	56	57	67	78
Resting heart rate (standing)	67	69	81	89
Treadmill endurance time (seconds)	671	659	524	369
Recovery heart rate (seconds)				
After 1 minute	73	77	82	104
After 4 minutes	66	65	76	91

It was no surprise to learn that runners—the marathoners and distance runners together—weighed less than those in the two control groups, had less body fat and lower resting heart rates, and could run longer and recover faster. It was interesting to note, however, that distance runners had a physical profile very similar to that of the marathoners. This confirmed what I'd always suspected—that you get a lot of benefit out of the first few miles of a run, but, in relation to the work you've put in, relatively little out of the last several.

The rest of the study concerned the menstrual cycle and confirmed what other studies had shown: that women in training had a higher incidence of menstrual dysfunction than normal. The sedentary controls menstruated an average of 11.5 times per year, the athletic controls 11.2, the distance runners 8.5, and we marathoners 7.8. (There's a good chance I pulled my group down somewhat. As of late 1979 I hadn't menstruated in more than two years.)

At the same time other studies, as well as a lot of empirical observation, indicate that a small but significant percentage of girls in heavy athletic training, particularly swimmers and tennis players, don't begin to menstruate or develop secondary sexual characteristics until somewhat later than their less active peers.

In both instances, the obvious reason is that estrogen, the hormone secreted by the ovaries that causes a woman to menstruate and a girl to enter puberty, isn't doing its job.

Two questions then: Why this menstrual dysfunction? Is it of any concern?

In regard to the first question, the Atlanta study came to no firm conclusions. It suggested at least two possibilities. First, there may be some relationship, as yet unknown, between the percentage of body fat and the ability of the ovaries to secrete estrogen. The second possibility is that adrenaline, which is present in large quantities in athletes because it helps prepare them for action, might in some way override or neutralize the estrogen that is secreted.

As for the second question, I don't really know the answer, but it doesn't bother me too much. I've said before that there's no reason for girls—or boys—to begin heavy training until their early or mid-teens, but my reasons aren't medical. I just don't think there's any rush. I believe strongly that kids can better spend their time in other ways.

The Atlanta study was reassuring for those of us already in training. It concluded, in part, "We find the female athlete responds readily, favorably, and predictably to the demands of endurance exercise training. . . . We believe . . . that cyclic menses and fertility, if desired, can be expected to return after a decrease in the rigor of training, gain in weight, and possibly appropriate drug therapy."

In the summer of 1979 Dr. Allan G. Charles, a gynecologist and obstetrician associated with the prestigious Michael Reese Hospital and Medical Center in Chicago, caused a minor stir when he claimed that women runners may be prone to uterine prolapse and stress incontinence, two conditions brought on by weak pelvic muscles. (A prolapsed uterus is a uterus that sags. In extreme cases it may penetrate the vagina. Stress incontinence is urine leakage caused by the pressure of a sagging uterus on the bladder.)

Dr. Charles said flatly, "Women are not built for jogging. The female pelvis is much wider than the male's. Further, the muscular and connective tissue supports of the female pelvis are often weakened by childbirth, and therefore the uterus is not well enough supported to withstand the repeated impact caused by heels striking ground."

His remarks were reprinted in several newspapers around the country and in at least one national magazine—and brought a swift rebuttal from Joan Ullyot, a woman, a mother, a marathoner, and a medical doctor whose specialty is exercise pathology.

Dr. Ullyot explained that while uterine prolapse and stress incontinence may well occur in older women who take up running for the first time after childbirth, both conditions are symptoms of weak pelvic muscles and not the cause of them. Further, many gynecologists and obstetricians recommend that their patients take up running after childbirth in order to strengthen the weakened muscles.

"I've had a lot of experience with women runners," she said, "and I've never heard of a case of a prolapsed uterus or stress incontinence in a trained runner. Quite the opposite. Women runners actually have tighter pelvic musculature than nonrunners. Dr. Charles is talking through his hat. He just doesn't like jogging."

Running is a constant process of breaking down and building up; that is why the hard-easy principle makes so much sense, and if it is done carefully and within limits, it can be of great benefit. It does, however, involve certain trade-offs, some of which I've just tried to suggest. It is not a panacea. (Then again, what is? Arthur Ashe, the tennis player, suffered a mild heart attack in the summer of 1979. He was thirty-six years old, had never smoked, and because of an extensive and rigorous training program was in better shape than all but a handful of players on the tour—certainly he was in better shape than any other player his age. The question he asks, of course, is how severe the attack would have been if he hadn't been in shape.)

Running is stressful, and nobody knows for sure just how stressful it is or what the long-range effects of prolonged distance training are. Sports medicine is a relatively new field, and most of the testing to date has been done with world-class athletes, who by definition are at the edge of the athletic spectrum. This leaves 99.9 percent of the country's runners perhaps wondering what their training is really doing to them. I happen to believe that if a reasonable schedule is followed, there's no reason for concern—I read the other day where there has been a 22 percent decline in heart-attack deaths in the United States since 1969, and while many factors were at work to produce that encouraging statistic, there can be no doubt that the growth of participant sports, particularly running, was a major one—but I don't think we'll really know for another ten years or so, when there will be sufficient data to analyze the long-term effects of running.

Running Pain and Injuries:
Prevention and
Treatment

About a year ago I watched a television special about athletic injuries, the treatment of which is a rapidly growing specialty in the health care field. The sport given the most coverage was running, and one of the key points made by the narrator was that sooner or later everyone who runs develops pain. That shocked me at first, but when I ran through a mental list of all my running friends, I realized the narrator was absolutely correct. Every runner I knew, including myself, either currently was running with pain or had experienced some type of pain in the past. I began to wonder if pain was an inevitable consequence of running, particularly since pain had been such a persistent part of my own running life. To find out if this was so, I needed answers to some questions, beginning with the most basic one of all: What is pain?

Ben Vaughan, a structural integrator who teaches Rolfing and is an associate of Dr. Stan Dawson, explained that the word *pain* is derived from Latin and Greek words meaning "penalty." He said that pain is simply a sign that something is wrong somewhere in the mind-body system. It's like the sound a fire alarm makes when there's smoke or fire. The idea of pain as penalty implies that pain is the result of an improper or inappropriate thought or action. Mistakes, in other words, are what cause pain.

127

The fire-alarm analogy made sense. In fact, it even explained something I previously hadn't understood. Early in my running career, I had taken an injection of cortisone, a common pain-killer for aches and pains in muscles and joints. I didn't think twice about it. The injection made the pain go away and I felt great. But Stan explained that using cortisone to stop pain is like turning off the fire alarm without bothering to put out the fire. It stops the noise, but it doesn't do a thing to correct the damage. In fact, if the fire—the pain—doesn't go away on its own, the pain-killer may result in even further damage. Bill Walton, the professional basketball player, recently publicly criticized his former club's management and team doctors for encouraging him and his teammates to play after taking pain-killing drugs. Walton felt, and I now agree, that this sort of treatment philosophy encourages athletes to avoid the penalty of their improper actions and to keep on acting improperly as well. Overall, this increases, rather than reduces, the extent of the injury.

This example, and others like it, also made me realize that different types of health practitioners have different attitudes about the treatment of sports injuries. I have been treated for pain by both traditional and nontraditional practitioners, and I've formed some rather strong opinions about what works best—at least for me. There are a lot of variables, which I'll discuss more fully later in this chapter, but I lean toward practitioners who, out of respect for the wisdom of the body, are conservative in their approach and resort to radical treatments such as drugs and surgery only as a last resort. Unfortunately, few medical doctors, unless they are specialists in sports medicine, think this way. Practitioners who work with athletes are, contrary to Walton's apparent experience, much more likely to suggest treatments such as therapeutic exercise, manipulation, or a change in technique in the sport itself than are most medical people. As a whole, they resort to surgery and drugs far less than their counterparts in general practice.

In order to understand why pain and running are so commonly linked, it's necessary to take another, more technical, look at the mechanics of running. In the previous chapter I talked about how running relates to stress, tension, the cardiovascular system, the endocrine system, the lungs, the kidneys, and the nervous system.

Now let's look at running and its effect on the musculoskeletal system (the muscles and bones).

When you run, your heart works overtime to increase the flow of blood, primarily because there is an increased demand by your muscles for oxygen, nutrients, and the removal of waste. Abnormal concentrations in your muscles of one waste in particular, lactic acid, can trigger pain. At the same time, some tissue damage is inevitable, which releases two more chemicals that are also known to cause pain, bradykinin and histamine. As you run, your muscles contract. During a muscle contraction, blood vessels are compressed, decreasing the flow of blood. As the muscle relaxes between contractions, blood flow increases. While the overall blood flow to your muscles as you run may be fifteen times the normal rate, the flow is low during contraction and high between contractions. Also, the smallest blood vessels, the capillaries, are all fully open when you exercise, but only 10 percent of them are open when you are at rest. (This, incidentally, explains in another way why you should warm up before you run hard—before interval workouts, for example—to allow time for the capillaries to open.)

When you stop exercising, then, there is an interesting combination of factors that could cause pain. Immediately after you stop running, your muscles are somewhat tighter than they are during normal rest, and this excess contraction decreases blood flow. Ninety percent of the capillaries again close off, and the three chemicals that can cause pain are trapped in your muscles. This is why you're often sore the day after you run, especially if you're just starting out.

But if you exercise regularly, the vascular system learns to compensate. It builds collateral circulation (sort of like adding alternate routes), and your blood vessels readily dilate (a four-lane expressway can carry more traffic than a two-lane country road). Then the blood flow is sufficient to carry away the waste products that cause pain after exercise. Similarly, sudden increases in mileage or speed will also trigger pain, because of the breakdown of cells and the subsequent release of toxic wastes.

While the Greeks and Romans equated "pain" with "penalty," they didn't say that penalties are always bad. There is good, constructive pain and there is bad pain. If you avoid or suppress pain, one of two things can happen; neither of them is very good. You can forfeit the tremendous benefit running affords, or you can encourage further injury. Pain is best understood in the context in which it occurs. This underscores the weakness of the medical philosophy that calls for suppressing symptoms at all costs. Pain, Stan Dawson said, is not *always* due to mistakes but, ironically, may develop as a result of appropriate action. This explains why pain should never be ignored. The body lets you know when something is wrong. And it also explains why I proposed a very gradual running program for beginners. When you first start to run, it would be naive not to anticipate some pain, but it would also be foolish not to investigate the cause of the pain and seek help with any pain that persists for more than two or three days.

Now let's take a look at your bones. As you run, you land on each foot roughly 800 times per mile, each time with a force two to four times your body weight. Each of these shocks must be absorbed by your bones and your ligaments—ligaments being the tissues that hold your bones together. Most of this force is taken by your feet. Your ankles, lower legs, knees, thighs, hips, pelvis, and lower back absorb most of the rest, although this force is actually distributed throughout your skeleton. Many running injuries are caused by the trauma these frequent footfalls transfer to bones and ligaments, especially those in the foot and leg.

Each of your feet is composed of twenty-six bones and is held together by a complex system of ligaments. Each time your foot strikes the ground, it goes through a movement called pronation, which allows your foot to absorb the shock most efficiently. The main structures of the foot are three arches (the medial longitudinal, the lateral longitudinal, and the transverse) that give it its great shock-absorbing capacity, and if your foot, for whatever reasons, loses its normal structure, its shock-absorbing capacity is usually reduced.

Lower-leg muscles slip under a cartilage pulley at the ankle called the retinaculum and attach themselves to the top and bottom of your foot. Improper muscle tone or improper muscle action can either cause or aggravate a structural problem in your foot. Just as an improperly balanced automobile wheel causes uneven tire wear, so can an improperly balanced lower leg or foot cause the joints in the foot or ankle to wear abnormally.

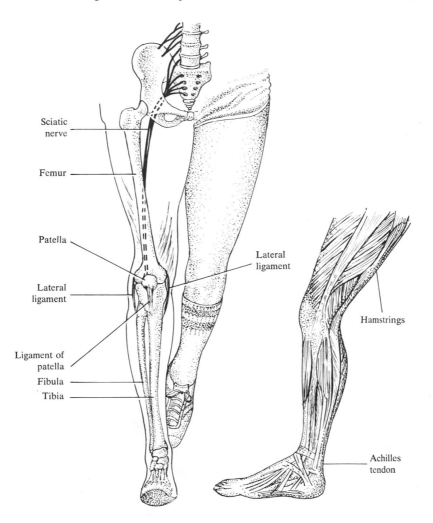

The runner's leg is a sturdy arrangement of muscles,
bones, ligaments, tendons, and nerves.

The ankle and knee are primarily hingelike joints. They should move in a very specific way when you run, so that there is no rotation of your leg, and they should move in a plane with the direction of your running. If the ankle or knee twists, there is a tendency toward increased wear and tear in these joints.

The hip, a ball-and-socket joint, is the most adaptable joint in the lower extremity. If your foot does not rest properly on the ground, compensation will most likely take place in your hip. But a distorted hip joint can in turn affect your pelvis and lower back. Thus, it's easy to see that problems with your feet, the mechanical foundation of a runner, can influence the structure of your body all the way up to your lower back. In fact, because of the interconnecting nature of the whole structure, any problem with one joint must affect all other joints of the structure above and below it.

To further complicate matters, the presence and nature of the nervous system make it necessary to look to the spine for the origin of structural problems as well. Bones are passive. They don't move by themselves. They are moved by muscles, and nerves control the movement of muscles. The nervous system is the control system of the body and the physical organ of the mind; it is the connecting link between the body and the mind that makes it possible to refer to the entire system as the bodymind.

In the last chapter I said that stress of any sort—physical, chemical, emotional, mental, and so on—may overwhelm the intelligence of the body, via the nervous system, and create tension in the mind-body system. No matter what the source of the tension, it will be reflected in the muscle system. Thus, anything from a bad diet to problems at work or in the home can affect the nervous system, making the muscle system—as well as other subsystems of the bodymind—susceptible to injury.

The bodily functions that we cannot consciously control are controlled by the autonomic nervous system, which is further divided into the sympathetic and parasympathetic nervous systems. Under stress, the sympathetic nervous system becomes more active. Your heart beats faster and you breathe more rapidly, your adrenal gland moves into high gear, and there is decreased blood flow to the organs in the abdomen and pelvis and increased blood flow to the organs in the chest and to the muscles you use when you run. This process begins even before you start to run. It is called the "fight or flight" response, and if this takes place and you *don't* fight or flee, it is like having your car's emergency brake on while you drive. It tears up your car's engine. No matter what causes the stress, the reaction is the same.

In our fast-paced society, this stress reaction is triggered more and more often. And if you check the health statistics, a lot of engines are obviously breaking down. Strokes, heart attacks, ulcers, hypertension, kidney failure, diabetes, all the chronic degenerative diseases, and even the common cold are often closely linked to stress.

When the stress reaction is triggered too often, the body reacts like a spring that's been stretched too far. It doesn't snap back. When the bodymind is weakened from this constant wear and tear, its muscles and bones are affected, simply because they are not part of the system.

Ben Vaughan explained that if you could look at yourself from the side, your ear canal, shoulder, hip, and knee should all be in the same vertical line, one that would drop straight down to your ankle. But when stress distorts your body structure, the tendency is for most of your body weight to shift forward over the balls of your feet. As your body shifts forward, your lower leg strains to keep your body from literally toppling over. Your knees lock, your pelvis tips forward, and the backs of your thighs tighten. In this position, your lower body is tight and braced and it cannot support your trunk. This puts excess strain on your lower back, and you use a lot of energy just trying to stand up. And the more energy you use maintaining your balance, the less there is left over for other work. Such as running. A person with a body distorted by stress cannot possibly handle the strain of distance running and will very likely develop back or leg pains.

The point of what might seem like an overlong digression from the topic at hand—running injuries—is that a large percentage of people have stress-related structural distortion and don't know it. For runners, this distortion can be as bad as high blood pressure is for heart patients. But runners, I think, are largely unaware that stress even causes structural problems. Runners are also unaware that structural imbalance predisposes their bodies to injury.

What's even worse, few medical doctors would admit the connection between stress and injury, and even fewer would know what to do about it. But sports medicine specialists, such as podiatrists, chiropractors, osteopaths, structural integrators, and physical therapists, are likely to understand these problems and what to do about them without resorting to surgery or drugs unless it is absolutely necessary. Very serious structural problems will probably require the attention of an orthopedist or a neurologist.

No matter whom you consult, choose carefully. One of the most important factors in the selection of a health practitioner is his or her professional skill. Just as important is the rapport between the doctor and patient. Knowing and trusting your doctor can enhance the therapeutic potential of the relationship. And, of course, a practitioner who is also a runner is best of all.

Most people wait until they have pain before they seek professional help. By then, more often than not, both the client and the professional are oriented toward suppressing the pain. This is an approach I heartily don't recommend. Instead, consider optimizing the health and balance of your body and mind even if you aren't right now experiencing any problems. By reducing stress and tension through some type of organized program, you can go a long way toward preventing structural imbalance. Meditation and relaxation training certainly are good areas to explore, as is systematic stretching (see Chapter 8). Don't wait for pain. Find a knowledgeable professional who can help you optimize body balance, then work on avoiding structural problems before they occur. An ounce of prevention, remember, is worth a pound of cure.

Now I want to discuss some common minor and major running injuries and their probable causes, propose some possible cures, and suggest ways to prevent them from happening again.

Blisters.   Blisters are the result of excessive friction, and they are caused by such things as ill-fitting shoes, a crinkle in your sock, or even moisture. (You may never experience a blister until you slop through a puddle on a particularly rainy day.) Don't break a blister unless it is so uncomfortable that you absolutely have to. Small blisters can be covered with three or four layers of gauze held in place by tape or a Band-Aid. Large blisters may have to be lanced. Puncture them carefully with a sterilized needle, drain the fluid, and apply a liberal dose of tincture of iodine or something similar. To help prevent blisters, make sure your shoes fit and that you put on your socks carefully—and to reduce friction also apply a generous helping of Vaseline or cold cream to the blister-prone areas.

Blisters are not serious unless they become infected or cause you to change your gait. If they make you run differently, don't run. If one becomes inflamed, see a doctor.

Black toes.   Discoloring of the toenail—actually the skin beneath the toenail—is a blood blister and is caused by excessive pressure on the nail. Blood blisters, too, are relatively harmless, except in extreme cases where the buildup of pressure is so great that the nail is forced away from the skin, in which case you may lose a toenail. You can sometimes lance this kind of blister yourself by probing beneath the nail with a sterilized needle or piercing it from the top. (A doctor would use a small drill.) But this won't be necessary if you take precautionary measures early on. Black toes most often occur because your shoe's toe box is too small or slopes too sharply. You may need a new pair of shoes, but as I suggested before, make some one-inch vertical slits, about one inch apart, over the top of the affected toes. This will usually relieve the pressure just enough for the problem to go away.

Bunions.   A bunion is an inflammation of the joint where the big toe joins the first metatarsal bone. (This joint is sometimes called the bunion joint.) The inflammation is the result of stress caused by the big toe's trying to bend under the first toe. Most bunions are merely uncomfortable when you walk, but almost all of them are painful when you run. The inflammation can be reduced by an orthotic pad—an orthotic being any device for the foot used to restore or maintain what Dr. Steven Subotnick, author of *The Running Foot Doctor*, calls a "functionally neutral position"—but in rare cases the only sure cure is surgery to straighten out the offending toe.

Calluses.   A callus is the thickening of the skin at those places where there is friction. Modern running shoes are so well padded that runners actually experience fewer of them than the general population, and in moderation they are of benefit. The thick buildup protects the skin from blisters and chafing; at the same time an excess buildup, which is usually found on the heel or on the ball of the foot, can also irritate the deeper skin tissues. If you are callus-prone, sand the calluses down regularly with pumice stone and apply Vaseline or skin cream before you run.

Stress fractures.   Most of these occur in the bones of the metatarsal arch—the arch above the ball of the foot—or in the large bones of the lower leg. They are hairline fractures, and they are the dickens to diagnose. Sometimes not even the best radiologist can spot them on his or her X-ray plates until there is a calcium buildup at the point of the fracture, meaning that the healing process is well under way. Further confusing the issue is their resemblance to skin splints, if the fracture is in the leg, or bone bruises, if the break is in the metatarsal arch. Once a stress fracture is diagnosed, however, it is imperative to cut back your running lest a full-fledged fracture develop. Consult a specialist about corrective shoe inserts. Often a simple insole will be enough to prevent a recurrence.

Shin splints.   These are inflammations resulting from a tear in the muscles or tendons in the front of the lower leg or the separation of the muscles and tendons from the bone. They are most prevalent among beginning runners and are caused by running too hard too fast and without proper warmup or by shoes that aren't properly flexible and transmit excessive shock along the top of the foot to the lower leg. If the fronts of your lower legs ache after a run—or before one—do a few stretches for the afflicted area (just lean with your back against a wall and your heels 12 inches from it, and while keeping your heels on the floor, repeatedly raise your toes toward you), and take care to ease gently into your runs.

Achilles tendinitis.   Tendinitis is an inflammation of a tendon and is caused by a tearing or stretching of the tendon itself. (The inflammation is the body's way of surrounding the injured tendon with protective fluids that deliver the nourishment necessary for its recovery.) Any tendon, of course, is subject to tendinitis—tennis elbow, a common lament, is an inflammation of the tendons in the elbow—but the Achilles tendon is a susceptible area for runners.

A healthy Achilles tendon, which connects the muscles on the calf to the heel, is indispensable to good running. Indeed, if you should ever sever your Achilles tendon, you wouldn't be able to walk. The symptoms of Achilles tendinitis are a severe soreness in the tendons, stiffness following a run, and an inability, because of pain, to run fast.

The causes are many. One is simply running too hard too fast and without warming up. Another is running in shoes without sufficiently raised heels. A third is a tightness of the calf muscles, which then tug on the tendon.

Likewise, the possible cures are many. You can do warm-ups that stretch the Achilles tendons and the calves, try a shoe insert that raises your heel, avoid sudden bursts of speed (even if this means curtailing your Fartlek runs and interval workouts for a while), or apply warm water to them before you run and ice afterward, to reduce the swelling. Also, stay off hills.

"Runner's knee." More properly called chondromalacia of the patella, or kneecap, runner's knee is the most common of all knee injuries, as knee injuries are the most common of all running injuries. It is a disintegration of the cartilage under the kneecap. The symptoms are a grinding feeling under the kneecap and a dull ache that begins shortly after you start running and gets worse as you continue.

The cause of runner's knee was a mystery for a long time. It was thought to be congenital, but the fact that it occurred so often among runners led doctors to look elsewhere—to the feet. It is now assumed that runner's knee is caused mainly by an improper foot plant and to a lesser degree by an imbalance between the resting muscles in the front of the upper leg and the working muscles in the back. In both instances, unnatural stress is transmitted to the knee.

Improper foot plant can mean many things. If, for example, you have Morton's Foot, a condition in which your big toe is abnormally short, your foot plant will no doubt be wobbly. A corrective foot support can possibly solve your problem.

If your feet pronate excessively, this might also be causing an excess stress that results in chondromalacia. In a perfectly balanced system, the top of your leg rests more or less directly over the bottom of your leg. But excessive pronation of the foot causes an inward twisting of the lower leg, and the lower leg was not designed to twist very much. The result? Your knee is exposed to a constant rotational stress, causing pain.

The solution can sometimes be simple. What you want to do is make your landing platform more stable and reduce pronation. One way is to build up the inside of the heels of your shoes by inserting a pad, thus, as I described in Chapter 3, making a homemade version of the varus wedge. In addition, doing exercises that strengthen your quadriceps, in order to bring them in balance with your hamstrings, can also relieve stress in the area of the knee.

Sciatica. This is an irritation of the sciatic nerve, which runs from the lower back down the legs and in mild cases is sometimes mistaken for a pulled hamstring. The main cause is a musculoskeletal

imbalance in the lower back or pelvis that can lead to impingement of the sciatic nerve or a decrease in the blood flow to the nerve itself.

Also, weak abdominal muscles, which put an excess burden on the muscles of the back, have been identified as a sciatic culprit. If this is diagnosed as the problem, do exercises that isolate the abdominal muscles and strengthen them while not also toning the back. One such exercise is called a sit-back. Hook your toes under something sturdy. Start in a sitting position with the knees bent. Lean back halfway to the floor and hold for 20 seconds. Repeat three times once per day.

Pulled muscles.   Muscle strains, pulls, and tears are all the same thing—a separation of muscle tissue that may result in a sharp initial pain and long-lasting soreness. What the separation is called is just a matter of degree, with strains being the least severe and tears the worst.

There are two basic causes. The first is putting the muscle in action too quickly and demanding too much of it. The second, again, is muscle imbalance, with untrained muscles putting too much of a burden on the trained ones. You can usually keep running with strained muscles if you take the basic precaution of warming up properly. Pulled muscles need rest and also ICE— Ice, Compression (in the form of a wrap like an Ace bandage), and Elevation—followed by a very gentle easing back into your running schedule. Torn muscles, if severe, may require a pain-killer such as cortisone to relieve excruciating discomfort. Don't ever consider training, however, if you've taken cortisone or any other similar medication. A pain-killer doesn't cure. It merely numbs the pain, and continued running could result in further damage.

Ankle sprains.   A sprain is a tear in the ligament. (Ligaments hold joints together; tendons connect muscle to bone.) A twisted ankle is usually caused by a freak accident and won't happen again unless you step into the same pothole. If your ankles collapse under you for no apparent reason, however, you might check out the wear in your heel counter. If it's too flexible, you may be courting another mishap. The immediate treatment is to elevate your leg and apply an ice pack. Rest is essential, for two or three days following a mild sprain, and for two months or longer after a severe one. In extreme cases, the damage cannot be repaired except by surgery.

Don't consider running until there is a complete absence of pain. Not only will you aggravate the injury, but your body will transfer as much weight as it can from the hurt foot to the healthy one. Your gait will change, shifting the stresses in your legs, and you will encourage another injury to show up somewhere else.

Cramps.   Not all running injuries are foot-related. Muscle cramps result when the blood is overextended and cannot both cool the body and supply muscles with the nourishment they need. According to Dr. David Costill, a prominent exercise physiologist, cramps are caused by fluid loss and by a depletion of the electrolyte reserves. (Electrolytes are minerals in the body that regulate cellular metabolism.)

If your legs cramp, you will, of course, be forced to stop running or at least be hobbled. Cramps are the muscle's way of announcing that the mind-body system is overextended. In the future, increase your fluid intake, and also check your diet for any nutritional deficiencies, particularly salt, calcium, magnesium, and potassium.

Side stitches.   While everybody in the world has experienced the symptoms of a side stitch—a stabbing pain of varying severity usually isolated near the bottom of the right side of the rib cage— nobody seems to know what it is. The best guess is that it's a spasm of the diaphragm muscle, which separates the lungs from the abdomen. There are four likely causes: general tension, unrhythmic breathing, running without a proper warm-up, and running on a full stomach, especially one loaded with hard-to-digest food. The only sure relief for a stitch is to stop running and do some deep belly breathing, and even that is not guaranteed to work. But in the future, give your food more time to digest, warm up carefully, breathe rhythmically, and, above all, relax.

Dehydration.   Chronic dehydration can be a problem during the summer months if you can't run early in the morning or late in the evening or if you live in a Sun Belt state, where there is nearly a year-round abundance of hot weather. Thirst is an unreliable guide for fluid regulation, and runners and other athletes replace only a fraction of the liquids they lose during a workout through sweating. If this loss is allowed to accumulate over several days, chronic dehydration is the result. You will feel fatigued, find it difficult to sweat, and the subsequent rise in your body temperature will put a strain on your circulation system. According to Dr. Costill, a two- or three-pound decrease in weight from day to day is a good warning of chronic dehydration, and you should go out of your way to take in extra fluids. Don't worry about drinking too much. Your kidneys will easily take care of the excess.

Heat exhaustion.   Dehydration is the primary cause of heat exhaustion. The symptoms are a cold and clammy feeling, pale skin, and nausea, and if you ignore them, you will become disoriented and finally faint. To treat heat exhaustion, immediately stop running, start taking in fluids—and get out of the sun. The most severe degree of heat exhaustion is heat stroke, which occurs when your body has no more fluids to lose. You will stop sweating, your skin will become prickly hot, you'll have difficulty breathing, and there will be a burning sensation in your chest. You will become disoriented and probably collapse. In which case, hope that somebody near you knows what to do. Heat stroke is an emergency, and without immediate attention the victim could go into a fatal coma. The first and only treatment is to immerse the victim in liquids—water, milk, or any safe liquid that's handy—in order to promote cooling by evaporation. Don't try to give liquids internally to a heat stroke victim. It won't do any good. The most effective treatment is to rub the victim liberally with ice cubes. Get him or her to a hospital immediately.

8

A Whole Body Workout

I took nine years of ballet when I was growing up, and several years of modern dance and tumbling as well. Off and on I played tennis, rode a bike, swam, and water-skied. I enjoyed all these participant sports and activities, and in high school and at the University of Georgia I was a cheerleader. My prerunning years, in short, were reasonably athletic.

When I started running, though, I pretty much stopped doing a lot of these other things. I didn't give them up entirely—except for cheerleading—but for five years I got most of my physical exercise on a running track or along a roadway.

Then a friend of mine suggested I join her exercise class.

Me? I knew my friend was well-meaning, but after all, I was running 4 or 5 miles per day. I was in the best shape of my life. Why would I want to do a lot of frilly exercises with a group of women who probably couldn't run once around the block?

But I went anyway, just to be polite.

I was the only woman in the class who couldn't touch her toes.

That was a revelation of the first order. I started to realize that in the process of getting reasonably good at running, I had created a significant imbalance in my body; that by focusing so narrowly on one area of physical conditioning, I had lost whatever skills I once might have had in others.

This was not terribly devastating news. I knew that if all I ever did for the rest of my life was keep on running regularly—that if I never again put on water skis or picked up a tennis racket—I would still be doing my body a great favor as well as helping my peace of mind. At the same time I wondered if there wasn't another kind of physical activity that would fill the gaps that my running-only program had created—and perhaps even improve my running as well.

There were two, as it turned out.

A well-rounded, healthy body is one that is durable, flexible, and strong. By itself, running improves endurance dramatically, but it increases strength only selectively and may actually retard flexibility—as my first trip to that exercise class showed.

Regarding flexibility, a distance runner's stride is short and lacking in variety. If you attempt to do anything with your legs that demands quickness or agility after you've been running distances for a good while, you're liable to be disappointed. As for strength, running does wonders for your heart and lungs, and for your lower body, but very little for the muscle systems in your upper body. To gain overall flexibility and strength—and to retain what you already have—you must look elsewhere.

There are several ways to improve flexibility. The easiest and simplest is through a short program of stretching.

Stretching has always been popular among runners as a way to warm up before a workout and cool down after one, but in the past several years it has gained acceptance by the nonrunning athletic community as well. High school, college, and professional sports teams, long burdened by the pulled muscles of their players, are turning to stretching as a way to cut down these, and related, injuries, and with encouraging results. Sometimes the task of getting a musclebound defensive lineman to agree to do some stretches is not an easy one, but on the other hand, who would have thought a few years ago that football player Alan Page, the all-pro defensive end, would make marathoning the centerpiece of his off-season conditioning program? Attitudes do change. At the same time stretching is beginning to replace the old, boring, potentially harmful, and fairly useless calisthenics favored for so long by school gym instructors and the general population alike.

Stretching, of course, can be a primary physical activity on its own. Yoga, for example, might be simply defined as advanced stretching with large doses of controlled breathing and meditation thrown in. Indeed, many of the stretches I'm about to describe are derived from classic yoga positions.

What stretching does figuratively is loosen up your muscles and the connecting tendons. What it does literally is increase the elastic range of a muscle or muscle group. Stretches should always be done slowly because when a muscle is jerked into extension, its natural reaction is to snap back and shorten itself. Whether you are stretching or running, this is when you can get hurt. But if you stretch correctly, two things happen. Your muscles become relaxed —and relaxation, remember, is one of the keys to good, efficient running—and they become more flexible, which reduces the possibility of soreness, strains, and pulls.

Let me take one common stretching exercise that all of you have done at some time in your life, toe touching—or trying to—and use that to explain the fundamentals.

Stand up, and spread your feet a shoulders' width apart. Keep your legs straight, and slowly bend over from the waist, extending your hands toward the floor only as far as you comfortably can— that is, when you feel a solid tension, or pulling, in the back of your legs. Depending on your suppleness, you might be able to place your hands flat on the floor, or you might not be able to reach much beyond your calves. It doesn't matter. The beauty of stretching, like running, is that it can be done at your own individual pace.

Hold this position for 15 to 20 seconds while relaxing as totally and as completely as possible. At no time during any stretch should your muscles shake or quiver, nor should you feel any pain —the tension of the stretch, yes, but no pain. The idea is to get your muscles to stretch themselves more or less voluntarily.

As you relax, the tension of the stretch will lessen and perhaps even go away entirely. Great. Now you are ready for the second part of the stretch. Reach farther toward your toes until you once again feel a solid tension in the back of your legs. Bob Anderson, the author of an excellent book on this subject called *Stretching,* identifies this second extension as the developmental part of the stretch. It is when improvement takes place and should be held at least as long as the first half of the stretch.

The key to a good stretch, I've found, is in your ability to relax, which is enhanced if you continue to breathe normally and easily and concentrate on the part of your body being stretched. Many beginners are tempted to hold their breath as they stretch, but this only creates excess tension, which tightens your whole system and reduces the effectiveness of the stretch. I find it particularly advantageous to exhale slowly as I enter the first half of a stretch.

If you have difficulty breathing, or if your muscles start quivering, you're either trying to do the stretch too quickly or attempting too much of one. Back off a bit, to a position you find comfortable.

One final comment before we move on. Whenever you do a stretch that involves bending at the waist from a standing position, as this one does, bend your knees slightly when you straighten up. This removes the burden of the ascent from your lower back, a troublesome area for many people, and places it on your legs.

There are hundreds of different stretches. Here are several of the many that are of particular benefit to runners. They are presented more or less in descending order, beginning with those for your neck and ending with those for your calves and Achilles tendons. They offer all the variety you need to increase the flexibility of all parts of your body. Don't be surprised if you become addicted to stretching. I did. From my embarrassing beginning I developed a series of stretching routines set to music and for several years taught them in the Atlanta area.

Unless otherwise noted, do all these stretches in two parts, holding each segment for 15 to 20 seconds.

Neck

1. This stretch is usually called a neck roll, but it really shouldn't be done in one continuous motion. Bend you head forward and tuck your chin until you feel the stretch in the back of your neck, and hold this position for 15 seconds. Now roll your head toward your right shoulder until you feel a good tension in the left side of your neck. Hold for 15 seconds. Then put your head back, close your mouth, and raise your chin until you feel the stretch in your throat, and hold for 15 seconds. Finally, roll your head toward your left shoulder, stopping when you feel tension in the right side of your neck; hold for 15 seconds. Relax with your chin

on your chest, and repeat this sequence in the opposite direction. This stretch especially helps dissolve the tension that often builds up in your neck after a long run.

Shoulders and arms

2. Place your left hand behind your head, and with it reach for your right shoulder. Place your right hand on your left elbow, and gently pull your elbow toward your right shoulder.

3. Place your left hand behind your head and your right hand behind your back. Now try to shake hands with yourself. At first, this stretch usually requires a towel. Once you can join hands, slowly pull down with your right hand to stretch your left shoulder. Repeat the stretch with the position of your hands reversed.

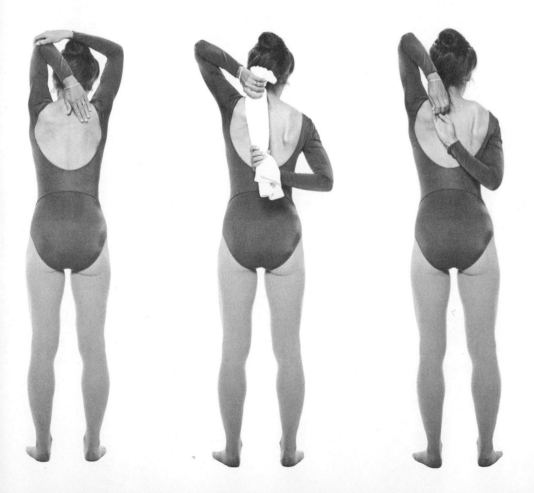

4. Grasp the ends of a towel waist-high in front of you, and slowly bring the towel over your head until it is waist-high behind you. You'll probably find it necessary to bend your elbows at first. When you can do this stretch without bending your elbows, place your hands closer together. Repeat ten times.

5. Clasp your hands waist-high behind your back. Keeping your elbows straight, slowly raise your hands until you feel the tension in your shoulders. Hold, and slowly lower your arms.

Lower back

6. Lie on your back with your arms extended at shoulder level and your head turned to the right. With your left hand grasp your right leg just above the knee. Now gently rotate your hips to the left. When you feel your right shoulder start to come up off the floor, hold. Repeat to the other side.

7. Stand erect with your feet spaced apart the width of your shoulders. Place your left arm against your left hip and thigh. Slowly raise your right arm over your head, and remembering to

breathe normally, bend your body as far as possible to the left while reaching over your head and then down toward your left side with your right arm. At the same time slide your left arm down your left leg toward the floor. Hold, and repeat to the other side.

8. Lie on your back with your arms extended at shoulder level. Draw up your knees to your chest. Now rotate your lower body to the left side as you turn your head to the right. Hold, return your head and knees to the center, and repeat to the other side.

9. From a sitting position, draw your knees to your chest; then clasp your hands around them. Place your chin on your chest from this egg-shaped position, and gently roll up and down on your spine eight to ten times.

10. Lie flat on your back with your hands on your hips. Bring your legs over your head as far as you comfortably can. Don't force your breathing. Depending on your suppleness, you might want to place your arms on the floor next to your sides or extend them behind your head. You might also try spreading your legs as you near the end of the stretch and placing your knees on either side of your head. This stretch, a classic, is called the plow.

Abdomen

11. The best exercise for strengthening abdominal muscles is a bent-knee sit-up. This is not really a stretch, but I'm describing it here because it's an exercise that every runner ought to have in his or her portfolio.

Lie on your back, and bend your knees so that your feet rest comfortably flat on the floor. In order of difficulty, you can rest your arms by your side—this is the easiest—cross your hands on your chest, or clasp your hands behind your head. Do whatever feels most comfortable. Curl your back until your shoulder blades are clear of the ground, and hold this position for 10 seconds. Repeat a half-dozen times.

The reason for this exercise is that running does very little for your abdominal muscles. Yet a weak abdomen forces the muscles of your lower back to assume a disproportionate amount of the responsibility for supporting your upper body. The minimum result is soreness; the maximum result could be a debilitating strain.

12. Lie on your back with your knees bent, and clasp your hands behind your head. Now curl your back, and draw your knees toward you. Then rhythmically alternate trying to touch your right elbow to your left knee and your left elbow to your right knee. Repeat ten times.

Groin

13. Sit on the floor and bring the soles of your feet together as close to the groin as possible. Straighten your back, hold your head up, and press the heels of your feet together.

14. Lie with your back on the floor and your legs resting against a wall. Split your legs, and while keeping your feet against the wall, lower them toward the floor. Place your hands on the inside of your thighs and gently press down.

15. From a comfortable standing position and with your feet pointed out approximately forty-five degrees, clasp your hands in front of you and slowly squat while keeping your heels flat on the floor. Use elbows to push knees apart; this stretches the groin area more. Hold. As you loosen up, increase the distance between your feet before you start your squat.

16. Sit erect with your feet extended in front of you and split your legs as wide as you comfortably can. Keeping your back straight and your feet flexed—toes pointed toward you, hands grasping toes—slowly bend forward. Do this stretch again, this time with your toes pointed away from you, hands grasping your ankles. If balance is a problem, put your hands on the floor in front of you.

Hamstrings

17. Stand erect with your feet 24 to 36 inches apart. Raise your arms to the level of your shoulders and extend them to either side, palms down. Slowly twist your body to the right, reaching toward your right foot with your left hand. At the same time, extend your right arm upward and turn your head to look at it. At first, you may be able to hold this position for only a few seconds, but keep working at it. Relax, and repeat to the other side.

18. Begin from a seated position with your legs extended together in front of you. Keeping your back straight, slowly reach for your toes and flex your feet. Keeping your head up will help you maintain a straight back. Another variation of this stretch is bending forward and keeping your elbows near the floor.

19. From the same seated starting position, bend your left leg until the sole of your foot touches the inside of your right thigh near the top. Now flex your right foot and reach toward it—head up and back straight—and hold. Relax and repeat to the other side. You can also try the variation of bending forward and keeping your elbows near the floor during this stretch while bending your left leg outward, as close to your thigh as possible.

20. Lie on your back with your legs resting on a wall, getting as close to the wall as you can while keeping your buttocks on the floor. Flex your kneecaps and your feet.

21. This stretch requires a waist-high table or counter top. Place your right leg on the object, and while keeping both legs straight, relax and slowly reach down your left leg with both arms as far as you comfortably can. Hold, relax, and repeat to the other side.

Quadriceps

22. Kneel with your toes pointing behind you. Bring your right leg forward and place your foot flat on the floor in front of you. Using your left hand for balance, reach back with your right hand and grab your left ankle, and gently pull it toward you. Hold, and repeat to the other side.

23. While standing about 2 feet away from a wall and using your left hand for balance, bend your right knee, and grab your right ankle with your right hand. Keeping your back straight, pull your foot toward your buttocks. Hold, and repeat to the other side. To intensify this stretch, bend slightly at the waist, and pull your foot up behind you as high as you possibly can.

24. The hurdler's stretch is a classic thigh exercise. Sit down with both legs in front of you. Keeping your right leg straight, bend your left leg beneath you as much as you can, or until your left foot tucks up against your left buttock. Using your hands for balance, lean backward until you feel a good stretch. If your knee comes up from the floor, however, you've gone too far. Repeat to the other side.

This is an excellent stretch, and from the ready position—with your foot tucked—you can lean forward and get an equally good hamstring stretch in the leg extended in front of you.

Calves and Achilles tendons

25. The basic lower-leg stretch is often called the "wall lean" and is the one most associated with running. Stand two or three feet from a wall or tree. Press against the support with your arms straight in front of you. Now place your right foot about 6 inches from the support. Keeping your heels flat and your left leg straight, move your hips toward the wall. To intensify the stretch, lift your right foot. With your left knee straight, the stretch most directly affects your left calf. You can transfer the stretch to your left Achilles tendon by slightly bending your left knee. Repeat to the other side.

26. Kneel with your toes pointed behind you, and slowly sit back on your ankles. Place your right foot even with your left knee, and raise your right heel 1 or 2 inches off the floor. Lean your chest on your right knee and thigh. As you create pressure on your knee and thigh, slowly lower your right heel. Repeat to the other side.

27. Stand on a high curbstone or step, with your right heel dangling over the edge. Lower your heel by slowly transferring weight to your right leg. If you keep your right leg straight, you'll stretch your right calf. If you bend your right knee, you'll transfer the stretch to your right Achilles tendon. Hold for 15 seconds, and repeat to the other side.

Not all stretches have to be done alone. Here are just three of several you can do with another person.

28. Sit opposite your partner with your legs and his or hers spread apart and the bottoms of your feet touching. Grab each other's forearms. Gently pull your partner toward you until he or she feels a good stretch in the groin, hamstrings, and lower back. Release your pull if you feel any quivering or excess tension in your partner's legs or arms. Hold for 20 seconds, and then let your partner pull you in a similar manner.

29. With your partner lying on her back, face her and kneel beside her on her left side, and put your hands on the floor just above the outside of her knees. Now place her right leg on your right shoulder. Slowly raise your partner's leg. At the same time your partner should gently push down with her raised leg. She will feel tension in both her right hamstring and lower back. At this point, hold the stretch for 20 seconds. Then stretch her other leg. Finally, switch positions with her.

30. As your partner lies on her back with the soles of her feet touching, kneel in front of her, and place your hands on the inside of her lower thighs. Gently push her legs toward the floor until she feels a stretching in her groin. Hold for 20 seconds, and reverse positions.

I've suggested only a handful of the possible stretches, but these should give you some idea of what this kind of exercising is all about.

Most runners make stretching a regular part of their workouts; all runners should. A top-notch pair of shoes and a good stretching routine afford the best possible protection against the vast majority of running injuries.

A complete routine that includes at least one stretch for each part of the body takes no more than 10 minutes to perform, often less. Experiment with the stretches I've described—or make up your own—and put together a sequence of your favorites. It might look something like this:

Begin with the *neck* roll (No. 1); then grab a towel, and do a *shoulder and arm* stretch (No. 4). Next, lie on your *back* with your arms extended at shoulder level and draw your knees to your chest. Rotate your lower body to the left as you turn your head to the right, and vice versa (No. 8). While still lying down, do a half-dozen bent-leg sit-ups (No. 11) to strengthen your *abdomen*; then, from a sitting position, bring the soles of your feet together (No. 13) to stretch your *groin*. Now straighten your legs and touch your toes (No. 18) to work your *hamstrings,* and move from there to the hurdler's stretch (No. 24) to test your *quadriceps.* Finally, stand on a step (No. 27), and loosen your *calves and Achilles tendons.*

I heartily recommend a routine similar to this both before and after a workout. You need to warm up before you run (although some runners prefer to jog slowly for 5 minutes or so before stretching out, and that's fine), and afterward a few stretches will ease the inevitable tension you've built up. If time is a problem and you can stretch only once, make sure it's after your run. I realize you may be more inclined to stretch beforehand—as I am, but a postrun stretch, when you're fully warmed up, has twice the benefit.

Of the three cornerstones of a well-rounded conditioning program, two are now firmly in place: running, which improves endurance, and stretching, which increases flexibility. Now it's time to discuss the third: weight training, which will build strength.

Weight training?

Yes.

When Ben, who had been training with weights for years, and still does, first suggested I try some lifting, I was pretty skeptical, to say the least. Weight training and running seemed to me an incompatible pairing—at the very least an incongruous one—and I resisted it for several years. But once I got started, it didn't take me long at all to become a staunch advocate.

At first glance, especially if what comes into view is one of those grotesquely massive heavyweight lifters you see on television from time to time, weight training would seem to bear very little relationship to running. And it's true that you could probably train to run in the Women's International without ever going near a barbell. (It's rumored that Bill Rodgers, the three-time winner of the Boston Marathon, cannot do even one simple pull-up.)

But let's divide the body in half, at the waist, and consider weight training from a fresh perspective. You, as a runner, obviously need strength in your lower body. Just as obviously, the simplest and easiest way for you to acquire it is by running, which, in fact, is what you do. Unless you have particularly weak leg muscles or are recovering from knee surgery, there is little need ever to consider extensive lower-body weight training. Besides, it interferes too much with your running. I've tried strapping weights on my ankles and doing some simple leg extenders, but I quickly found that the only concrete result was a big hole in my basic hard-easy training schedule. If I lifted weights with my legs on an easy day, that turned it into a hard day; lifting leg weights on a hard day was impossible. I learned that I could build all the leg strength I needed by doing a few extra interval workouts, especially on a slope—for example, by striding uphill a quarter-mile or a half-mile and slowly jogging down. Doing that about eight times in a row was plenty.

The upper body, however, is another matter entirely because from a strength standpoint, running largely ignores it. Thus, a moderate upper-body weight-training program can be of tremendous help in keeping both halves of your body in balance. It also helps increase muscle tone in all parts of your body.

Furthermore, despite the great number of very good runners around who are shallow-chested, I'm convinced that upper-body weight training can be of great benefit—to all runners. I suggested earlier that your body is like a machine, with your legs being the

wheels and your arms the engine, and that if you could just keep your arms pumping even when your wheels were a little tired, you would continue to move at a steady clip. Increasing your upper-body strength, in moderation, can't help improving the ability of your engine to work.

With that in mind, let's begin.

I have used all sorts of weight-training equipment, including the elaborate and expensive machines found in health clubs, but before you join a local spa or the YMCA or YWCA in pursuit of such equipment, check with your husband, boyfriend, brother, or some other friendly male. One of them might have a set of dusty barbells lying around in his basement somewhere, and they will be just perfect for your purposes. (Failing that, you can buy a standard set of barbells for about $30.)

A basic barbell set consists of a bar that weighs approximately 15 pounds and around 40 pounds of lead weight plates, the lightest being 2½ pounds, that can be added to or subtracted from the bar at will.

The weight-training schedule I'm about to outline is designed to increase strength in your shoulders, chest, back, and arms, and to improve overall flexibility. It is not meant to build muscle bulk, which in women it would have a hard time doing anyway because we usually lack the necessary quantity of the muscle-building hormone, testosterone.

1. *The military press.* The primary muscle groups involved in this lift are those of the shoulders. Standing before a full-length mirror in order to be sure you center your pickup of the bar as you should each time you work with weights, keep your feet spread beneath the bar a shoulders' width apart. Keeping your back erect —as you should do every time you pick up the bar—bend your knees and waist and grasp the bar, palms down, with your hands also spaced a shoulders' width apart. With your back still erect, straighten up and lift the bar to a resting position in front of your shoulders (your palms should now be facing up) with your elbows tucked into your sides. Without arching your back, push—or press —the bar directly overhead until your arms are fully extended. Then lower it to your shoulders and repeat.

2. *The upright row*.   In front of a full-length mirror, grasp the bar in the same manner, but with your hands only 6 to 8 inches apart. Being careful to keep your back straight, stand up. The bar will be hanging about waist-high. Keep your palms down, and lift the bar to just under your chin. As you do so, spread your arms so that at the top of the lift your elbows are flared and slightly higher than the bar. Then lower the bar to your waist. This lift strengthens your shoulders and your trapezius, the primary muscle of your neck.

3. *The bench press*.   The pectorals—the chest muscles—are the primary beneficiaries of this exercise. Lie on your back on a raised

bench, and lower the bar to your chest with your hands spread slightly more than a shoulders' width apart. Push up until your arms are fully extended, and return the bar to your chest. This lift is more easily done if you have a partner nearby to help you position the weight properly.

4. *The bent-over row.*   Before the mirror, stand with your feet slightly more than a shoulders' width apart and directly under the bar. Bend over as you did for the military press, and grasp the bar with your hands palms down and directly over your feet. Keep your knees and waist bent. With your elbows next to the outside of your knees, lift the bar to your chest, and return it to the floor. This lift particularly affects the latissimus dorsi: the primary muscle of the lower back.

5. *The barbell curl.* With your feet a shoulders' width apart and directly under the bar, bend and grasp the bar with your hands palms up and placed just over your feet. Check yourself in the

mirror to be sure your pickup is centered. When you stand up, the bar will hang below your waist. Now curl the bar to your chest by bending your elbows. Keep your elbows near your sides, but don't tuck them. That's cheating. This lift is the mirror image of the upright row and benefits your biceps, the major muscles in the front of your upper arms.

6. *The tricep curl.* The triceps are the muscles in the back of your upper arm, and in women they have a tendency to become flabby, mainly from disuse. Stand with your feet beneath the bar and spread a shoulders' width apart. Glancing in a mirror to center your pickup, grasp the bar with your hands palms down and spaced 6 inches apart. Bring the weight to a position directly over your head,

and fully extend your arms. Keeping your elbows high, lower the bar behind your neck. Then straighten your elbows to return the bar directly overhead.

There are three simple rules to keep in mind as you begin your program of weight training.

First, warm up properly, just as you would before a run. Do some stretches—picking a sequence similar to the one I described earlier in the chapter—and then try a few push-ups. To do a full push-up, lie on your stomach, and raise yourself with your arms, keeping your back and legs rigid. If this is too difficult at first, settle for a half-push-up, in which your knees remain on the ground.

Second, maintain good form. Do the lifts exactly as I have described them, and do them smoothly. Lift the weight in two counts, and in two counts return it to the resting position. It is very important to use a floor-length mirror to observe whether your pickup of the bar is properly centered and balanced.

Third, breathe in rhythm with your lifts. Exhale as you lift the weight (or, in the case of the tricep curl, as you lower it), and inhale as you return it to the resting position.

The number of times you do each lift depends on what you are trying to accomplish and how much weight there is on the bar. Weight-training experts agree that using heavy weights that permit only a small number of repetitions—between four and six—results in the greatest gain in strength and muscle size. Using lighter weights that allow more repetitions—between eight and fourteen —also promote strength, but there is a minimum increase in muscle size. That is what I prefer.

Now for the big question: How much weight do you lift?

As much as you can, but it's a little more complicated than that.

Put on just enough weight so you can comfortably do the maximum number of repetitions—fourteen—and still have something left when you're finished. For some of the lifts, you might be able to do the fourteen repetitions only if you use just the bar. Fine. Take your time.

Now add more weight, just enough to lower the number of repetitions you can do without strain to eight. Stay with that weight until you once again can do fourteen repetitions, and then begin the sequence again.

Each lift, of course, requires a different weight. The tricep curl will probably take the least number of pounds, and the bench press the most.

All this probably sounds very complicated, and until you get the hang of it, it is. The answer is to experiment. The ability to lift weights varies dramatically from one person to the next, just as does the ability to run or stretch. Some of you may run out of weights the first day—you can easily add to your collection—while others of you won't be able to lift much more than the bar for a while. Proceed at your own pace.

It took me about two weeks of hearty trial and error before I got my starting weights for all six lifts squared away, but after that I found I could make the necessary adjustments and readjustments quickly and routinely.

Once you master this weight-training program, you can breeze through all six lifts in about 20 minutes. Weight training does not need to be done more than three times per week, and I personally prefer lifting on my easy-run days, or on those days when I don't have any running scheduled at all.

In addition to stretching and weight training, there are all sorts of other physical activities that will both complement and enhance your running. A couple of hours of tennis, racquetball, or other sports that emphasize agility, quickness, and hand-to-eye coordination, for example, provide a nice change of pace from your regular training. So do swimming, cycling, and cross-country skiing, the last being a sport with which I've absolutely fallen in love. Besides, many runners go a little crazy if they can't get in their regular runs, and having a sport in reserve is often a nice substitute when an injury or bad weather makes your regular workout impossible.

By now you are probably muttering to yourself that all these extracurricular activities sound just fine, but how on earth can you fit them into your day? Well, it does sound like a lot, and in some respects it is. You'll have to decide for yourself how much of this you can, or should, undertake. But consider: if you are near the end of the running schedule outlined in Chapter 5, and if you do the stretches before and after each of your five weekly workouts, train with weights three times per week, and indulge in a second sport for a couple of hours a week—if, in short, you do absolutely everything I've suggested you do—you'll still be spending fewer than 75 minutes per day in enjoyable pursuit of a healthy life. Considering the return, I think you'll agree it's a small investment of your time.

9

Energetic
Eating

One of the secondary reasons why I took up running was to lose weight. In college, and even before then, I was an inveterate nosher, and in my heart of hearts I still am. I love snacks, and if nobody's watching, I head for the ice-cream parlor as soon as I finish a run. I've even taken to having Ben hide some of my favorite munchies—health food cookies, sesame butter, gorp, and the like —so I can't yield to my temptations. Then I get mad when he won't tell me where they are.

I'm not really too unusual in this respect. People who run a lot think they can eat anything. For every dozen runners who count their calories and balance their proportions right down to the last bean sprout of their carefully wrought diet, you'll always find one who trains on Twinkies and Coke or some other such concoction and gets away with it. It is rumored, and not too forcefully denied, for example, that Frank Shorter downed a six-pack of beer the night before his run in the marathon at the 1972 Olympics. It was his rather pleasant way of giving himself one final shot of carbo-hydrates before his grand and successful effort. But remember, you lose only about 100 calories for every mile you run, and unless you have a very unusual metabolism, you earn that back with a few bites of a gooey candy bar or some healthy swigs of a chocolate malt. The only way to lose weight is to reduce the amount of food you eat.

In one sense, I suppose, you should do as I say and not as I do —or at least not as I want to do—when it comes to dietary matters. I'm 5 feet 5½ inches tall and I weigh 120 pounds. According to Dr. Irwin Maxwell Stillman of diet-book fame, the average weight for a woman my height is 127½ pounds. According to a simple formula devised by Dr. Stillman, however, my ideal weight is 115 pounds. And my ideal *running* weight, as calculated by Dr. van Aaken, is 102 pounds. (For women, Dr. Stillman's average weight chart starts with a base of 5 feet and 100 pounds. For each inch of height, add 5 pounds. For men, the base figures are 5 feet and 110 pounds, and then add 5½ pounds per inch. To figure your ideal weight according to Dr. Stillman, subtract 10 percent of your poundage. To calculate your ideal running weight according to the rather strict Dr. van Aaken, subtract 20 percent.)

These charts, and others like them, have their value. They provide workable guidelines, and they suggest what most Americans, at least, have never quite been able to accept—that when it comes to food, we are one of the more indulgent societies around. However, after years of trial-and-error experimentation, I have come to the conclusion that everybody has an ideal weight, but one that may or may not fall within the parameters of any of the accepted guidelines. I am reasonably happy with my 120 pounds. Although I wouldn't mind dropping an additional 3 or 4, I am fairly certain that I would be uncomfortable if I dropped much below the recommended 115, and I know for a fact that I would be weak and unable to run anywhere near my capacity if I plunged to 102. Women worry about their weight, especially when they go on a diet and lose a lot of weight easily and quickly and then find it hard to lose any more. I don't really believe they should get too upset. A certain number of pounds will come off easily and naturally. When losing weight starts to hurt—figuratively speaking, of course—take it as a sign that your body is settling into its natural weight, and don't fret.

I sometimes think I've tried every diet under the sun, faddish and otherwise. At one time I lived on milk shakes with raw eggs mixed in because that's what seemed to work for Ben. When the price of beef began to skyrocket a few years ago, we both eliminated red meat from our diets—more, I should admit, for reasons

of economy than anything else. I could go on and on. In the end, I came to three conclusions about diets.

First, most of them are too extreme in one way or another, and you are continually robbing Peter to pay Paul. When I stopped eating red meat, for example, I found that while this made life easier for my digestive system, it also made me too weak. I needed protein from somewhere, and I apparently wasn't taking in enough from other protein-rich foods to make up for what I was losing through my abstinence from beef.

Second, while most diets, especially the popular, faddish ones, are a superb way to lose weight, they are an absolutely terrible way to keep weight off. This is mainly because if you deviate from it in the slightest way, you quickly gain back most of the pounds you've lost. Weight-*loss* diets are not weight-*maintenance* diets, and there is a big difference.

Third, diets tend to be tedious. Many runners are practicing, conscientious vegetarians, and that is fine—I lean that way myself. But by making a fetish of their diets, they tend to spend their entire day eating one carefully planned meal and then figuring out the logistics of obtaining the ingredients for the next one. If you travel a lot, as I do, you can't always count on finding a friendly neighborhood health food store or restaurant in the lobby of your hotel.

But if you're careful, and—here's that phrase again—listen to your body, you can discover for yourself the nutritional principles that lead to a diet that is both healthy and enjoyable. When that happens, it will hardly seem you're dieting at all, and in a sense you won't be. One definition of the word *diet* is "eating by prescribed rules." If the rules are so easy to follow that you don't have to pay any attention to them, can it really be said you're dieting?

I don't pretend to be an expert on nutrition. On the other hand, after having read extensively on the subject, and after several years of experimentation, I'm not terribly convinced anybody is. The whole subject is a mine field dotted with controversy and confusion, and about the only point of agreement is that relatively little is known about it.

To illustrate, I recently heard of an experiment in which laboratory rats were fed all of the known nutrients—and still suffered from malnutrition. The only conclusion the researchers could come up with is that there are a bunch of nutrients out there that haven't yet been isolated and identified.

On a more practical level, you can read bumper stickers announcing, "Milk Is for Lovers," listen to commercial jingles that say, "Milk is a natural," and find experts who pronounce that milk is the ideal food, a complete protein that's rich in calcium, builds strong bones, and prevents tooth decay. But you can also find an opposite set of pundits who argue that milk is mucus-forming (bad), that many adults lack the enzyme to digest it, and that we humans are the only species of animal that drinks milk after it has been weaned—in short, that drinking milk is not only unhealthy, it's unnatural as well. What are we to do?

Specific food items aren't the only source of confusion. The avalanche of diet books, each one advertising the ideal diet for *you,* only serves to muddle the soup, as it were. I am more and more convinced that no single diet is right for anyone except the original person for which it was designed.

Dr. Roger Williams has pointed out that each one of us is biochemically unique. Consequently, we each digest food differently and need different kinds of food to replenish ourselves.

A truck driver has different nutritional needs than a secretary. On a practical level, where you live and the seasons of the year have a lot to do with what's even available to eat. A lazy summer dinner in New Orleans differs mightily from a Christmas feast in Minneapolis.

So I'm not going to burden you with my version of the "ideal" runner's diet. I would, however, like to discuss in a general way some aspects of diet and nutrition that might help you, as a health-conscious runner, decide the best way to eat.

Let me begin by expanding on what I said a moment ago about weight-loss diets. In general, they are not good health-maintenance diets, nor do they help much when you've reached your desired weight. Many weight-loss diets are low in calories, but the amount you eat while losing weight is obviously not enough to maintain your ideal weight. Once you reach your desired weight, you need to return to a normal—for you—amount of food. In addition, weight-loss diets are often high in protein and low in complex

carbohydrates such as grains, fruits, and vegetables. But authorities such as Paavo Airola and Dr. Henry Bieler recommend just the opposite kind of diet—one that is low in protein and high in complex carbohydrates.

The fresher the food, the greater its nutritional value, and as any organic gardener will quickly tell you, fresh food also tastes better. Corn on the cob is an obvious example. If corn is not eaten within an hour after it's been picked, it goes through chemical changes that make it taste less sweet. It also undergoes a change in texture, from crisp and crunchy to dull and mushy.

The mood you're in when you eat affects the value you get from a meal. I discussed earlier the autonomic nervous system and what happens to it under stress—namely, that the activity in the sympathetic nervous system picks up and dominates the parasympathetic. This, in turn, reduces the flow of blood to abdominal organs such as the stomach, small intestine, liver, colon, pancreas, and gall bladder. When this happens, the production of hydrochloric acid in the stomach is reduced, and the peristaltic contractions, which move food through the intestinal tract, become weaker and take place less frequently. In short, if you are tense and upset when you sit down to eat, you will digest food inefficiently and assimilate less of it. But if you are relaxed and happy at the dinner table, you'll digest your food easily and you will be better able to assimilate it. It's true that you are what you eat, but it's even more true that you are what you assimilate.

Blessing the food you're about to eat also helps your mood. By willingly acknowledging the Creator and the miracle that His food is to us, you will affect your autonomic nervous system. This isn't anything you can fake. You have to actually think and feel gratitude. In a very subtle way, blessing your food also enhances its value. If, for example, the cooks at a restaurant are upset for one reason or another when they handle your food, blessing the food can help to neutralize that negativity. I can understand if all of this sounds a bit like mumbo-jumbo, but a certain segment of the scientific community believes a researcher's mood has a very real effect on the outcome of his or her controlled, apparently objective experiments. If a scientist's mood can affect cold facts, then a cook's mood can certainly affect the way he or she prepares a hot meal.

It's no great secret that Americans eat too much—all you have to do is look around you to see the truth of this. Obesity is a disease of epidemic proportions. But we are also inclined to overcook our food, with generally poor results. Cooking breaks down fiber and makes food easier to digest, but at the same time it may break down the enzymes and vitamins that are essential to the digestive process, thus decreasing the overall value of the food. Even if you're not a runner, you could probably stand to eat a lot more raw food, especially vegetables and fruits. Or, if you insist on cooking your food—certain foods, obviously, have to be cooked —consider only lightly steaming it. This method of cooking, I think, greatly enhances the flavor of certain foods, especially vegetables, and also avoids an excessive loss of vitamins and enzymes.

Cooking oils make food harder to digest. When heated, certain chemical bonds of oils and fats are strengthened and require an excess of energy to break. Oils and fats are broken down in the small intestine by bile from the liver, via the gall bladder and with the help of pancreatic enzymes. They are then absorbed in the small intestine and head for the lymph glands or the bloodstream. In either case, they eventually pass through the liver, where the process of digestion is completed. The stronger the chemical bonds in the oils and fats, the harder the liver has to work, which is why fried foods are notoriously hard to digest. So give your liver a break tonight. Eat less, cook less, and don't ever fry anything.

Certain foods should be avoided entirely, including refined sugar and flour, salt, coffee, tea, and soft drinks. Sugar and white flour are refined carbohydrates that contain empty calories with absolutely no nutritional value. When raw sugarcane and whole wheat are refined, the fiber, vitamins, and minerals are processed away to leave "pure" white sugar and white flour. Pure, in this case, does not mean wholesome. Since the vitamins are gone, when you digest sugar or flour your body must rob the B vitamins necessary for digestion—as well as other chemical goodies—from somewhere else, and an excess of sugar and flour can actually lead to B vitamin deficiencies, which in turn can affect your mental and physical health. (One of the leading causes of schizophrenia is now thought to be B vitamin deficiency.) Try raw honey and whole-grain flour instead.

There are at least three good reasons for avoiding common table salt. The body is composed of cells that live in a fluid environment similar in mineral content to that of the ocean. Certain minerals are found in greater concentration inside the cells; certain others outside the cells—among them sodium and chlorine, which are what salt is made of. Wherever there is a large concentration of minerals, water is drawn to that spot to balance things out. When you add salt to your diet and thus to your body, water moves from the inside to the outside of your cells, and the result is dehydration. Also, table salt is processed at extremely high temperatures, making it difficult for the body to assimilate. Finally, when there is an excess of salt in your system, your kidneys must work overtime in order to eliminate that excess. Enough? As a substitute, try vegetable salt or sea salt that has been processed at low temperatures.

Coffee, tea, cocoa, chocolate, and cola drinks all contain caffeine, which puts stress on your body because it stimulates your nervous system, a fact that everybody who depends on a cup of coffee or two for a "starter-upper" in the morning well realizes. There are several good coffee substitutes on the market today. Or try herbal teas, hot carob drink, hot apple cider with cinnamon and cloves, or other drinks that don't contain caffeine. If you're not crazy about the idea of giving up your coffee, try a little experiment. Stop drinking it. If you have headaches for the first two or three days of your abstinence, be assured that your body is mildly addicted to caffeine. Next, go on the coffee wagon for two weeks and then pour yourself a cup. Now note your racing heart, your sweating, your anxiety, and your general inability to relax. It should be clear that you don't need that influence on your system.

Eat only when you're hungry. The purpose of eating—the only purpose—is to provide your body with high-quality tissue-building material with which it can replace dead and dying cells. Food is energy with a purpose, and when we eat for any other reason we confuse our bodies. Often we eat only to indulge our taste buds or in order to satisfy or suppress some mental or emotional state. Or we eat because it is "time" for lunch or dinner.

But your body doesn't really know or care what the time of day is, and if you listen to it, the only real signal it will give you regarding food is that it's hungry. Most people have never experienced true hunger. They eat before they get truly hungry, or for other irrelevant reasons, and they eat too much.

Try another experiment. See if you can recognize what you *need* to eat rather than what you *want* to eat. And try to undereat systematically. Observe how you feel. Listen to your body. Assume that it knows best regarding what and when you should eat, and how much. If you listen, eventually your body will dictate a nice, regular, rational diet. What you need to eat will come to equal what you want to eat.

As you experiment with your diet, you might also find that you're allergic to certain foods. A quick way to find out—courtesy of Dr. Arthur Coca in his book *Pulse Test*—is to take your pulse just before eating a particular food and once again right after you've finished. If your pulse rate increases by 8 to 10 beats per minute or more, the chances are good you're allergic to it. As our environment becomes more toxic, more and more people are developing food allergies (as well as other kinds of allergies), sometimes without even suspecting the cause. And as life becomes more stressful, the same thing happens.

There's a connection. Environmental toxins trigger a stress reaction. When this happens, your stomach reduces its production of hydrochloric acid, which helps break down protein. When protein is not completely broken down, more stress to finish the job is placed on your liver, which then gets clogged with undigested protein. Your liver becomes less able to perform certain other tasks, one of which is to control the amount of histidine and histamine in circulation. Histamine is the substance that seems to irritate the nasal passages and cause mucus flow. At the same time, your bronchial tubes become constricted. Between the two, there is a greater chance of obstruction, infection, or both. If this sounds like the symptoms of asthma, hay fever, and other common allergies, it should.

What's the point of all this? The liver, as I've suggested, is responsible for detoxifying environmental toxins. Food additives, such as preservatives, fillers, and dyes, are often toxins. But just as you can tell in two weeks' time what the caffeine in coffee and tea does to your system, so, through Dr. Coca's pulse test, can you perhaps find out what your body's response is to certain other foods, especially those with additives in them.

Many runners have become vegetarians, or, like myself, near vegetarians. For us, life begins after meat. There are thought to be twenty-six amino acids, twelve of which must be eaten every day because the body doesn't manufacture them. Red meat is an excellent source of these amino acids, but so are sprouts, nuts, seeds, beans, grains, dairy products, and a whole bunch of other things. These nonmeat protein sources are generally easier to digest (the notable exception being certain milk products), and they are also cheaper, more energy-efficient, and less toxic. A wonderful book, Frances Lappe's *Diet for a Small Planet,* teaches how to combine foods to obtain complete protein from nonmeat sources.

Most meat is full of environmental toxins, as well as animal waste, drugs, dyes, and additives. Processed meats are the worst. Even those of us who aren't 100 percent vegetarians could stand to cut back on our meat consumption. Our water supplies are in trouble, too, and many people are beginning to see the wisdom of drinking only spring-bottled water.

One of the many controversial areas regarding diet concerns nutritional supplements. Do we need them? The answer is a definite maybe. It depends on a lot of variables, the main ones being whether we're getting the tissue-building materials we need from the food we eat and whether our bodies are working well enough to assimilate enough of the stuff it does have access to.

Runners have special nutritional needs because they burn up certain things that more sedentary folks don't. A runner needs glucose, which is best gotten from complex carbohydrates. The adrenal gland of a runner puts out a substance that affects the kidneys, which, because of what I noted earlier, means that salt intake should be restricted and potassium intake increased. The adrenal also needs more vitamin A, vitamin E, riboflavin (a B vitamin), and vitamin F. An active pituitary gland requires protein, vitamin E, riboflavin, choline, and pantothenic acid to help prevent adrenal exhaustion. Vitamin C helps in detoxification and with cortisone metabolism.

It all gets very confusing, and my best advice here is to consult a nutritional counselor. I take a lot of supplements, whether or not I know for sure that I need them. I consider them an inexpensive insurance policy.

Finally, research your medical heritage. This is so obvious that it almost goes without saying, yet few people do it. There is a history of multiple sclerosis in my family, for example, and there is some evidence that MS is caused, in part, by the absence of minerals, especially magnesium. Magnesium is one of the minerals that is used up under stress, and for that reason I make it a point to add foods rich in it, such as green vegetables, apples, seeds, and nuts, to my diet.

A more common hereditary problem is heart disease, which is exacerbated by hypertension, or high blood pressure. One way to reduce high blood pressure is to avoid coffee and tea and the other caffeine-loaded beverages as well as common table salt.

If obesity lurks in your family tree, consider a diet that's high in complex carbohydrates.

This sort of thing is nothing more than common sense, and while good eating habits won't necessarily immunize you from the hereditary sins of your fathers and mothers, a proper diet might well help minimize the problems lurking in your family tree.

If all of this sounds terribly dogmatic, I apologize, because that's not my intention. Not long ago, Ben and I went camping in Colorado for a week. We were served huge steaks three nights running. This was more steak than we'd eaten at home in the previous three years, but we enjoyed every bite and we didn't hesitate to clean our plates. If we are invited to a dinner party, we don't screen the menu in advance, and if we're at a buffet where every item on the table is loaded down with things we would normally avoid, we don't go away hungry.

The point is that once you've established good eating habits, if you fall off the table every now and again it won't hurt you any more than missing a day's running will hurt your overall conditioning. Just as you should let running serve you rather than the other way around, so should your diet be flexible enough for you to enjoy without guilt the occasional meal that might not otherwise meet your standards. Don't be a prisoner of routine, and don't hesitate to experiment.

10

Running
and Beauty

I'm always surprised when people come up to Ben and me at camps, clinics, and races and remark how refreshing it is to see a couple of distance runners who actually look reasonably normal. Most of the runners they've seen before are gaunt, sallow, weathered, anemic types. "And," they ask, especially if they are women, "am I going to wind up looking like that if I keep running?"

The answer, of course, is a resounding no. It is quite possible, and rather easy, to run as hard and as fast as you can and still look nice.

What is beauty anyhow? Certainly it is in the eye of the beholder, and just as certainly the standards for judging it have changed and changed back many times. The trend over the past couple of decades has been to associate good looks, in both men and women, with outdoor, physical activities of the sort that gives your skin that healthy, rosy-cheeked look. The woman who is proud of her body and does everything she reasonably can to keep it well toned through exercise has it all over those who succumb to the sedentary life. And the same goes for men, too.

It is very easy, however, to go overboard in the pursuit of health and beauty. For example, one of the main reasons why people take up running is to lose weight. At the same time not many of us, including myself, have a natural runner's physique. Lucky folks

179

Runners must work to protect their skin and hair from the elements.

like Frank Shorter, Bill Rodgers, and Miki Gorman—the last of whom stands 5 feet 2 inches tall, weighs just 94 pounds, and has been a top marathoner for more than seven years, although in 1980 she will celebrate her forty-fifth birthday—don't have to work hard to lose weight. The rest of us do. Typically, a woman is a little bit

Miki Gorman in Japan.

over her normal weight and very much over her ideal weight when she begins to run, and almost immediately she changes her diet. She reads somewhere that red meat is bad for a runner and somewhere else that meat of any kind ought to be avoided, and before she knows it, she's a full-fledged vegetarian. Which is fine. What isn't good is that the chances are better than fifty-fifty that she hasn't reached the part yet where the author talks about keeping your diet balanced no matter what you eat. By not eating meat, she eliminates a main source of protein, which her body needs to repair itself. Consequently her skin starts to lose collagen—a building block—and begins to sag. She has missed the point.

I suppose a simple definition of beauty care would be those things one does to compensate for the aging process. While the aging process obviously cannot be arrested, it can be retarded. Aging is caused by many factors, all of which contrive to prevent our bodies from replacing worn-out cells with new cells of equal quality. Overall this is not something we can do a whole lot about, although regular exercise and a proper diet do provide good first-line defenses. One kind of exercise—running—is what this book is all about; the importance of nutrition I have discussed in previous chapters. Considered this way, it seems obvious that beauty is fundamentally a matter of life-style and encompasses everything from how we work and play to what we eat.

While this suggests that beauty *is* more than skin-deep, it is nonetheless true that skin care—and hair care—are of particular concern to a runner, or any other person, who spends an hour or two each day exposed to the sun and the wind. Indeed, the primary purpose of the thriving cosmetics industry is to restore to our skin and hair that which the sun and wind taketh away.

Which is water.

As nearly all beauty experts maintain, beauty *is* water. All the hair conditioners, skin moisturizers, sunscreens, cold creams, and other beauty products on the market are there for two reasons: first, to prevent water from escaping from our skin and hair; second, to replace it quickly and efficiently when it does get away.

Sun and wind both remove water. Sunlight is also destructive because it contains powerful ultraviolet rays. In order to protect the deeper layers of flesh, the outermost layers of skin build up defenses, which we call a suntan. While a little bit of sun is fine,

frequent exposure to it produces a harsh, horny protective layer which dries out and becomes tough, wrinkly, and hidelike.

Check this out for yourself. No matter what your age, compare the texture of your facial skin, which has been exposed to some sun and wind no matter where you live or what you do, with the skin on an unexposed area that rarely feels these effects. There's no comparison.

What you can do about all this depends somewhat on the seasons and where you live—there's an obvious difference between the dry air and brilliant sun of a Rocky Mountain winter and the suffocating humidity of a Houston summer—but let me suggest a daily beauty routine for the woman who wants to spend an hour or two outdoors every day without doing more than minimal damage to her skin and hair.

I begin each day by splashing cold water on my face, just to wake up and get the circulation going. Then I wash my face with a water-based skin cleanser that is pH-balanced. (pH is a measure of the skin's relative acidity and alkalinity. Most skin is slightly acidic; most soaps are slightly alkaline. A cleanser that is pH-balanced simply has an acidity that more nearly matches that of your skin.)

After that I apply a moisturizer, which contains a carrier agent that actually puts back into the skin some of the water it has lost through evaporation. This is the key step in my beauty regimen, or anyone else's, and if you are going to spend lavishly on only a single item in your cosmetics kit, this is where to do it. A good moisturizer also provides the best base for any makeup I may wish to apply.

Apply your moisturizer throughout the day and specifically just before your run, right after it, and before you go to bed. The most important application, of course, is the one before your workout. Don't limit yourself only to your face. Cosmetic care involves your entire body. If you have naturally dry skin, lather the parts of your body that will be exposed, and pay particular attention to your lower legs, which seem to dry out more quickly than almost any other part of one's body. Moisturizers have a tendency to make you perspire more, but it's nothing to worry about.

Use a sunscreen—which a good moisturizer will contain—and if the sun promises to be particularly harsh, don't hesitate to use a sun block. (A sunscreen filters the burning rays; a sun block filters the tanning rays as well.) To protect against chapped lips, a lip gloss is never a bad idea. Also consider that visor I mentioned back in Chapter 3—anything at all to keep excess sun from your face.

Shampoo cleans hair, and conditioners replace the natural oils, which give it body and luster, that the shampoo has removed. Most shampoos have a conditioning agent built in, and for women with short haircuts, this is usually enough to prevent their hair from frizzing after a shower even if it is washed daily. But those of us with long hair need a separate conditioner to replace those lost oils simply because the ends are much older and thus considerably drier than the hair nearest the scalp. I wash my hair every other day—I don't have the patience to shampoo it any more often than that—and as with my skin cleanser, I look for a shampoo that is pH-balanced.

Running with long hair can be a pain, frankly. It blows in your face and chafes your neck, but if you just twist it into a ponytail and secure it with a barrette, you can minimize much of the discomfort.

If you have a long run scheduled, note those parts of your body where you have experienced chafing, and apply to them a generous coating of Vaseline or cold cream. One such area, for example, might be your groin, where the rubbing of your shorts or underwear can result in rawness. Another is the inside of your upper arm, especially if you wear a singlet. Women's singlets are cut higher than men's, and occasionally you might find your arms rubbing against the singlet's border or seam. I used to have a terrible problem with chafing from my bra right in the center of my breastbone. The only solution turned out to be equipmental rather than cosmetic; I switched to a leotard or a tank top, especially on my long-run days.

Finally, your feet. If you have been running regularly for any length of time, there's a good chance that your once-dainty feet, fit to be properly displayed in open-toe sandals, have acquired their fair share of blisters, calluses, and black toes. There are several ways to minimize these less than attractive problems and possibly even do away with them entirely. In regard to calluses— to repeat what I said earlier—use a pumice stone to keep them sanded down. If your shoes fit properly, you won't need the tough protection that calluses provide. As for black toes and blisters, after you've once again checked your shoes to make sure they fit, put a good heavy cream on your toes and between them to cut down the friction caused by the slight movement of your foot inside your shoe, and also make doubly sure that there aren't any wrinkles in your socks. This won't be a serious problem on short runs, but if you're on the road for an hour or more, you could be courting disaster. At the very least, you'll have to stop your run to rearrange your footwear; at worst, you'll find yourself hobbling home in pain. And that's not very pretty either.

The start
of the 1978
Avon Women's
International
Marathon
in Atlanta.

11

The Marathon Experience

So you want to run a marathon.

The first question to ask yourself is: Why? If you are able to follow the ninth month of Schedule II, you are already getting most, and probably all, of the physical and mental benefits that running has to offer. The additional time and effort that training for a marathon requires will yield slim rewards and, considering the

stresses involved, may even be counterproductive. And if you think the actual running of the marathon is fun, you are probably in for a slight surprise. While training for the race is enjoyable, and being able to say you've run one is also nice, the actual run is often fairly uncomfortable.

Why do it, then? That's a question you'll have to answer for yourself, but even after you've run a few, there's no guarantee that your answer, whatever it is, will make any sense—even to you. For me, there have been three overriding reasons.

First, although I have tried to suggest throughout this book that the reasons for running have little to do with setting records or being able to enter races, human nature being what it is, we sometimes need firm goals to help us maintain the mental discipline necessary to meet long-term objectives. In Chapter 5 I suggested that gearing yourself up for a 10,000-meter race, or even a fun run over a shorter distance, is a good way to make sure you get in your run on those days when maybe you'd rather be doing something else. Well, deciding to run a marathon—roughly four times the distance of a 10,000-meter race—is simply an extension of that. I know several runners who train rigorously for the marathon and have yet to enter one. They simply use that faraway goal to help them do what they've already decided is good for them— namely, run regularly. I can honestly say that I could train for six months in preparation for a particular marathon and not be upset if some unforeseen circumstance made me miss it. Sure, I would be disappointed, but I would also be out on the road the next day or as soon as I could.

Second, there is a certain mystique about the marathon. It is a classic distance, it probably gets more attention from the press than any other single track and field event with the possible exception of the mile run, and for me, anyway, it is the showcase competition of the Olympic Games, although there isn't an Olympic marathon for women—yet. There's nothing quite like assembling at the starting line for a marathon, whether it's the one in Boston on Patriot's Day or the local all-comers' race where the only spectators are friends of the family.

Third, marathoning sets you apart from most other runners. Once you cross that finish line and get your time, not only will you feel a great sense of accomplishment, but you'll know precisely where you stand in relationship to every other marathoner in the country—even the world—from Joan Benoit, who won at Boston in 1979, and Kim Merritt right down to your next-door neighbor.

Joan Benoit wins at Boston, 1979.
She is presently ranked the number-one American woman marathoner.

There are few undertakings in life where your place in the overall scheme of things can be measured with such accuracy and finality.

All in all, marathoning is worthwhile. Give it a go if you're so inclined. You just might surprise yourself.

Of course, not every runner is interested in the marathon distance, nor should he or she be. But let's assume that you are—for whatever reasons—and, further, that you've reached the point where you can do the workouts outlined for Month Nine of Schedule II with relative ease.

Find a marathon that's scheduled approximately nine months in the future. That may seem a long way off, but it will probably take you that long to progress from the point where you are now to the level at which you'll need to be in order to run it comfortably. Also, this will give you a goal and help focus your training.

Seek out a running partner with a similar goal, somebody who will keep you company and prod you on those days when you might feel iffy about the whole venture. (Of course, you will perform a similar task for him or her, too.) This will not necessarily be easy. I'm fortunate to have Ben as a running mate, and most of the time we train well together. It stands to reason, though, that any two runners are, over the course of several months, going to train at different levels. But with a little patience and understanding, this doesn't have to be a problem. I've trained with male runners who have better marathon times than I, but only in about two workouts in seven do they leave me behind. The rest of the time they are willing to slow their pace just enough to let me keep up, and it doesn't seem to hurt them at all. Similarly I can easily gear down—in distance training you nearly always run well within yourself anyway—in the company of slower runners without hurting my workouts.

During the nine months leading to your first marathon, keep reminding yourself how worthwhile your training is. Distance running is mental—at least 40 percent—and the longer the distance, the more you will need to draw upon simple, old-fashioned willpower. The goal you've set will help you in your training, and conversely, as we shall see, the fact that you've been diligent in your training will help you complete the race.

Finally, outline a schedule for yourself that's reasonable and comfortable. I am occasionally asked what the difference is between training for a 10,000-meter race and training for a marathon. The answer: not that much.

In 1972, you'll recall, I ran my first marathon and had a terrible time. It was slow and painful, and at the end of it I asked myself, *Can marathoning really be worth all that effort?* Two years later I ran my first real marathon—one for which I had actually trained —in 3 hours, 6 minutes, an improvement of more than an hour. What happened was that Tim Singleton, the president of the Atlanta Track Club, had explained to me that the only difference between training for a marathon and training for a shorter-distance race was the one long run per week. The rest of my training, he said, could stay pretty much the same. I followed his advice, slowly building to where I could cover 18 to 20 miles during my long run, and finished that 1974 marathon feeling as good as I have ever felt since at the end of one. Ben had a similar experience.

Since then both of us have refined our training. We've added hill work and interval work and other kinds of speed work and all sorts of variations on these. Although I've lowered my personal record by another 22 minutes since then, I attribute most of that drop to experience rather than an improvement in my training program. Almost without exception, the more elaborate my schedules got, the more they left me dying. At the same time, when I have been forced by outside circumstances to curtail my training —as I was before the 1978 Boston Marathon—I have turned in times way out of proportion to the intensity of my training.

I'm not suggesting you can run a marathon cold or even that you would feel comfortable running one if you followed the training routine proposed in Schedule II. On the other hand, I don't believe you need to put in 80, 90, or 100 miles or more per week in order to enjoy one. My third schedule, then, proposes to do just two things: increase your weekly base from just under 30 miles to no more than 50, and expand your long run from 80 minutes to 160. That, and some mental toughness, will bring you to the starting line of your first marathon in fine shape and to the finish line eager for more. Last and far from least, it's a schedule that demands the fewest disruptions in your life-style.

Schedule III

Month One
Run five days per week.
        Day One—45 minutes.
        Day Two—30 minutes.
        Day Three—45 minutes of Fartlek.
        Day Four—30 minutes.
        Day Five—90 minutes.

Month Two
Run five days per week.
        Day One—45 minutes.
        Day Two—30 minutes.
        Day Three—45 minutes of Fartlek.
        Day Four—30 minutes.
        Day Five—100 minutes.

Month Three
Run five days per week.
        Day One—45 minutes.
        Day Two—30 minutes.
        Day Three—45 minutes of Fartlek.
        Day Four—30 minutes.
        Day Five—110 minutes.

Month Four
Run six days per week.
        Day One—45 minutes.
        Day Two—30 minutes.
        Day Three—45 minutes of Fartlek.
        Day Four—30 minutes.
        Day Five—110 minutes.
        Day Six—30 minutes.

Month Five
Run six days per week.
>   Day One—60 minutes.
>   Day Two—30 minutes.
>   Day Three—45 minutes of Fartlek.
>   Day Four—30 minutes.
>   Day Five—120 minutes.
>   Day Six—30 minutes.

Month Six
Run six days per week.
>   Day One—70 minutes.
>   Day Two—30 minutes.
>   Day Three—45 minutes of Fartlek.
>   Day Four—30 minutes.
>   Day Five—140 minutes.
>   Day Six—30 minutes.

Month Seven
Run six days per week.
>   Day One—80 minutes.
>   Day Two—30 minutes.
>   Day Three—60 minutes of Fartlek or intervals.
>   Day Four—30 minutes.
>   Day Five—150 minutes.
>   Day Six—30 minutes.

Month Eight
Run six days per week.
>   Day One—90 minutes.
>   Day Two—30 minutes.
>   Day Three—60 minutes of intervals.
>   Day Four—30 minutes.
>   Day Five—160 minutes.
>   Day Six—30 minutes.

Month Nine
Run six days per week.
        Day One—90 minutes.
        Day Two—30 minutes.
        Day Three—60 minutes of intervals.
        Day Four—30 minutes.
        Day Five—160 minutes.
        Day Six—30 minutes.

This month's schedule is the same as for Month Eight.

If this schedule reminds you of Schedule II, it should, because it contains all the same principles. The schedule has one long run per week and one day of speed work per week, and it alternates hard and easy workouts. The only significant difference between the two timetables is one of degree. At the end of this one you will be running 400 minutes per week, your long run will be up to an impressive 160 minutes, and beginning with Month Four you will have only one day off to play with. I would suggest resting completely the day after your long run, but if you want to take off some other time, feel free. It depends only on how you feel, and the choice is yours. And if you're feeling stale, take a break of three or four days. It won't set you back at all.

There are several items worth noting, and in some cases repeating:

•   This schedule, like the others, is presented in terms of minutes per workout rather than in terms of distance. Don't let your mileage-oriented friends confuse you. One of the keys to successful marathoning—and by that I mean being able to complete the course in relative comfort—is simply putting in your time in order to build a solid foundation. While speed is certainly important, it ranks below your ability to stay the course—a matter of quantity over quality.

Besides, once you finish this schedule, you will have been running for at least eighteen months and should have a pretty good idea of your pace, which will make it easy for you to measure your performance in terms of both time and distance. For example, if you are a 9-minute miler—a reasonable expectation but hardly a requirement—you will be running 45 miles per week and covering a fraction under 18 miles on your long run; if you are an 8-minute miler, your weekly mileage will be 50, and your long-run mileage precisely 20. It's easy to go back and forth, but for right now think *time,* not *distance.* If you put in your time, distance will take care of itself.

• Speed work. I don't have any interval workouts listed until the third trimester of this schedule. This is because I don't like them very much—to have the best effect they should be done at a running track, and a workout at a running track bores me to tears nine times in ten—and if you choose to do Fartlek on all your speed days, you won't get any argument from me. Interval training, however, is good for you. It's more intense than Fartlek, and more disciplined, and one of the objects of this schedule is to create mental toughness in yourself.

Of the many different interval workouts, let me describe five:

INTERVAL A—Run 440 yards and jog 220 yards. Do this sequence twelve times.

INTERVAL B—Run 880 yards and jog 440 yards. Do this sequence eight times.

INTERVAL C—Run 440 yards, jog 220 yards; run 880 yards, jog 440 yards; run 1,320 yards, jog 440 yards; run one mile, jog 440 yards. Repeat this sequence once more, from the top.

INTERVAL D—Run 440 yards, jog 110 yards; run 880 yards, jog 220 yards; run 1,320 yards, jog 440 yards; run one mile, jog 440 yards; run one mile, jog 440 yards; run 1,320 yards, jog 440 yards; run 880 yards, jog 220 yards; run 440 yards, jog 110 yards. This one is tough. Ease up or cut it short if you feel it's too much.

INTERVAL E—Run 1 mile, and jog 440 yards. Do this sequence a total of five times.

These intervals should be done in exactly the same way as those I described in Chapter 5. Run at a speed about halfway between your normal pace and flat out, and shuffle along during your jogs so that you almost—but not quite—recover completely before starting to run again. But keep in mind that the important part of interval training is the running, not the length of the recovery jogs. If you're not recovering sufficiently—your pulse should drop to around 110, although this will vary from runner to runner—keep on jogging until you do. And don't forget your warm-ups and cool-downs.

Here is how I would suggest dropping the intervals into your schedule. During Month Seven, do Fartlek the first week, Interval A the second, Fartlek the third, and Interval B the fourth.

During Month Eight, do Interval A the first week, Interval C the second, Interval B the third, and Interval D the fourth.

During Month Nine, do Interval E the first week, Interval D the second, Interval A the third, and Interval E the fourth. (There is, of course, an extra week on the calendar every three months. This is free time, at least on your speed day. Pick whichever interval you want, or make one up.)

• The importance of the one long run each week cannot be overemphasized. Each week's training program revolves around it, and the entire schedule is designed to increase your endurance sufficiently so that you can run those 160 minutes—or 18 to 20 miles—regularly and easily. The beauty of this schedule, I think, is that it allows you to build a foundation and at the same time leaves you something in reserve so that the long run isn't a painful grind. Other training schedules I've tried, ones that emphasize greater mileage and more intense weekday workouts, left me drained and washed out even before I started on my long run. But when I've cut back my training to a schedule that more nearly resembles this one, I've found that my long run once again became the joy it always should have been.

Also, do your long run on the flattest course you can find. Save the hills for your midweek workouts.

• For all my dos and don'ts—or at least strong suggestions—this schedule can and should be as flexible as possible. While this one does require more discipline than Schedule II, it is still important for you to listen to your body as you run—indeed, considering the increased stress, even more so. Make every reasonable effort to complete your long runs, but if your body says no, don't hesitate to stop or walk for a while—and add on the lost time somewhere else. Conversely, if you feel strong on a given day, keep on going. But be prepared to cut short a workout, as long as it's not your long run, later on.

I have planned this schedule on the assumption you would begin it as soon as you finished Schedule II. If, however, you have been hovering around the end of Schedule II for several months, you might want to intensify your training by spending only two or three weeks on each of the nine segments. Let your body be your guide—and your mind as well.

One way to add variety to your running is by working out twice a day. This doesn't mean adding more training; it's just that some people like to split their daily runs in two. If you are doing awesome amounts of mileage, this makes sense, but I hate even to mention the subject here because there really isn't any place in this schedule for twice-a-days. During Months Eight and Nine, for example, you'll be running 30 minutes per day three times per week, and there's no point in breaking that up. Another day is reserved for speed work, and you don't want to compromise your intervals. A fifth day is given over to your long run, and nothing should interfere with it. Which leaves your 90-minute run on Day One. So, if you want to experiment, do a good 30 minutes some morning, and follow it up with another solid 60 in the late afternoon. But in general, don't worry about twice-a-days. At least not anytime soon.

Now it's time to make your marathoning debut. Be judicious in your choice of races. The field should be neither too small nor too large—ideally it should contain between 700 and 2,000 runners. Any more than that, and you might be unnecessarily caught up in the hoopla that surrounds a large marathon; any fewer, and you will probably find yourself running alone most of the time. There is an increasing number of women-only marathons, but for your first time out I would recommend a mixed field—only because it will be hard to find a women's marathon with a sufficient number of entrants.

Pick a course that's flat. A hilly course can be devastating the first time out, as I discovered, and even one that's slightly downhill presents problems that are better solved after you've gotten some experience under your belt.

Make sure the course is certified by the AAU—the Amateur Athletic Union—to be the correct marathon distance of 26 miles, 385 yards. Not too long ago there was a marathon in New Zealand where several runners turned in absolutely fabulous times—so fabulous that the course was remeasured. It was found to be about

1,200 yards short. That wasn't much, but conceivably a world's record could have been set had the course been the correct length. Of course, nothing counted. Make sure your first marathon time is a valid one.

There are four kinds of courses. There is a multiple-loop course, in which you cover the same ground two, three, or even four times. Avoid these like the plague if you can. Seeing the same scenery, and knowing you're going to see it again, is always boring and usually depressing, and because you'll be crossing the "finish" line so often, you just might be tempted to drop out before the end. Then there are out-and-back courses, in which you run approximately 13 miles in one direction, turn around, and follow the same roads back. These aren't too terrible, but they're not as good as a single-loop course, where you start and finish at the same place. But the best kind of course is a point-to-point course, in which you start at Point A and finish 26 miles, 385 yards later at Point B. The Boston Marathon is held on such a course and is the kind I recommend simply because you'll always encounter new landmarks and there will be less temptation and opportunity to drop out.

Two weeks before the race, which ideally will be two weeks after you've completed Month Nine, start to cut back your training. The first week, do your normal speed work and get in your long run, but on the other four days, reduce your runs by about 25 percent. Your schedule will then look something like this:

Monday—Run 75 minutes.
Tuesday—Run 25 minutes.
Wednesday—Do 60 minutes of the interval of your choice.
Thursday—Run 25 minutes.
Friday—Run 25 minutes.
Saturday—Run 160 minutes.
Sunday—Rest.

Assuming the race will be held on a Saturday, there are two theories about how to train the last week. Many runners prefer to rest entirely on Wednesday, Thursday, and Friday. But I like to work out lightly the day before a marathon, as I do the day before a 10,000-meter run, just to keep in touch with myself and stay loose. I do, however, cut most of my workouts in half and dispense with intervals. The long run, of course, is the race itself. Your schedule the week of the race, then, will look like this:

Monday—Run 45 minutes.
Tuesday—Run 15 minutes.
Wednesday—Run 30 minutes.
Thursday—Rest.
Friday—Run a slow, easy mile and take 10 to 15 minutes to do it. Really goof off, or take a long walk.
Saturday—Race.
Sunday—Walk and run for 30 to 40 minutes at a very leisurely pace. This is totally optional, and play it by ear, but a slow run the day after a marathon does help ease the aches and pains.

As race day draws near, increase your fluid intake. Beginning no later than Thursday, sip an extra two or three glasses of fruit juice, herbal tea, diluted fruit juice, prepared drinks such as Gatorade or ERG, or just plain water, even if you're not particularly thirsty. Extra fluids aren't all that important in a 10,000-meter race, but in a marathon they are crucial.

As a general rule, don't change anything about your regular diet. At some point, however, you might want to consider carbohydrate loading, a dietary fad currently in vogue among many marathoners. Although I don't carbohydrate load myself and some nutritional authorities believe its effects are largely psychological, it does have its adherents.

Being easily accessible, carbohydrates are the first fuel store your body turns to when you run. But your body has only a given supply of them; any excess is converted to stores of fat. This supply usually runs out after 20 miles, and the purpose of carbohydrate loading is to increase your given supply temporarily.

This supply is controlled by hormones dispensed by the endocrine system. If there are not enough carbohydrates present, these hormones call for replacements, and if the supply is severely depleted, they ask for more than they normally would. The idea, then, is to create a carbohydrate shortage so severe that your body will want to store a surplus when you finally provide it with some. If you load properly, according to some tests, you can significantly increase your available carbohydrate supply.

Your last long training run the weekend before the race partly depletes the store. To reduce it further, switch to a high-protein diet for seventy-two hours after your last long run, and avoid carbohydrates almost entirely. Then on the Wednesday before your race, switch to a diet rich in complex carbohydrates. This doesn't mean you should overeat, but you can indulge in pizza, pancakes, and all the other foods you've been denying yourself because you thought they were bad for you.

But a firm word of warning: don't carbohydrate-load for the first time before your first marathon. Practice it, if you'd like, once or twice several weeks, even months, in advance, substituting your long training run for the marathon. If you're careful, carbohydrate loading shouldn't adversely affect you. But it might, and it would be a shame to find this out the week of the race. Do your experimenting—all your experimenting—in practice.

The night before the race enjoy a plate of spaghetti even if you're not loading and, if it suits you, a couple of beers. Drink two or three extra glasses of liquid, and get a good night's sleep.

After a light, easily digestible breakfast on race morning, get to the starting line about an hour before the gun is scheduled to go off. This will give you time to park your car, get your race number, and otherwise check everything out. Will the race officials be giving splits? How often? Will the course be totally closed to traffic, or will only one or two lanes be blocked off for the runners? How many aid stations will there be, and where are their locations? What will they be serving? If you're not a particular fan of most commercial replacement fluids, which is what you'll probably be offered, you might want to volunteer some friends to give you what you do like at strategic intervals. (Conversely, be wary of what spectators offer. I once took from a well-meaning fan a swig of what I thought was ERG. It turned out to be a flat cup of Coke.) If you have any questions, seek out the race officials and get them answered.

I assume that you have already familiarized yourself with the course, either by car or perhaps on a bicycle—just as you did before your 10,000-meter race—noting the hills, the turns (yes, marathoners do occasionally take wrong turns), and any other significant aspects of the terrain. Note particularly the landmarks at the 1-, 5-, 10-, and 20-mile markers. These will be your most significant checkpoints during the race.

I said that at most 10,000-meter races there seem to be only forty or fifty runners who warm up properly. At marathons there are even fewer, and I don't understand why. Warm up exactly as you would for a 10,000-meter race or any other kind of race. Run a solid mile—the first third at a good jog, the second third a little faster, and the last third at almost your race pace—until you start to feel your second wind. Then do some good stretches, and head for the starting line.

Use this time—the hour before the race—to start getting yourself in gear mentally as well as physically. There will be a lot of things during the race over which you will have little control, but right now you control everything—your equipment, for example. A crinkle in your sock is no big deal during a short race, but in a marathon it would be devastating. Did you put your socks on smoothly? Are your shoelaces double-tied? Have you taken care of those parts of your body where you might have some chafing? The list is endless, and after the race I suspect you'll wish you'd thought of some more.

Determine what your pace will be before the race, and try not to deviate from it. Plan to run your first marathon at your training pace, perhaps a little slower and certainly no faster. If, for example, you can do your long runs at a 9-minute-per-mile pace, this will bring you home in just under 4 hours. If your training pace is 8 minutes per mile, you'll be at the finish line in just over 3 hours, 30 minutes. Whatever speed you set for yourself, you will want to cover the last mile in exactly the same number of minutes as the first. This is very difficult to do, even for the best runners, because obviously your *effort* in the last mile is going to be greater than in the first, but that is your goal.

Overall the real mental trick is to think of the marathon as two races—the first one 20 miles long and the second one 10,000 meters long. This way, if you reach the 20-mile mark feeling strong and having exerted a minimum effort, you'll know you can make it the last 10,000 meters. (Some runners think the reverse—that the marathon is a 10,000-meter race followed by a 20-miler. The theory is that once they've covered 10,000 meters, all that remains is the long run they've been knocking off with such easy regularity the past several weeks. It sounds reasonable, but I prefer psyching myself the other way.)

The start.   When the gun goes off, you'll be charged up and feeling wonderful. It's hard not to be emotional or nervous at the starting line, but try. Concentrate on getting away cleanly, without too much elbow banging, and settle into your pace as quickly as you can. Relax.

One mile.   Check your pace carefully. Listen for your split, look at your watch—if you're carrying one—or ask another runner for the time. It's too early to tell much about what's going to happen, but you should be firmly settled in and not running over your limit.

A breathtaking view of the start of the 1978 New York City Marathon, as seen from the top of the Verrazano Narrows Bridge, and a closer look at the early surge.

Five miles. This is your first serious checkpoint. No matter how you feel at the start of a marathon, you won't really know what kind of race you're going to have until you're well into it. You can feel great at the start and have some chronic problem turn up that will make the day miserable. Or you can feel sluggish and disinterested, and suddenly everything will clear up and you'll have a fine run. Right now is when all this begins to sort itself out.

How is your pace? If you're a little behind, don't worry too much. If you're ahead of schedule, however, slow down. Also, you should be going over your style checklist, especially if you feel a little uncomfortable. Are you overstriding? Is your arm swing nice and compact? Is your back erect?

Judy Leydig and I complete the first loop
of the 1978 Women's International in Germany.

Finally, this is probably where the first of the aid stations will be. Drink up, whether you think you need something or not. The way to drink during a marathon is to stop, pick up your glass, down the liquid, and then move on. This may seem more than basic, but drinking on the run, while flashier, usually results in a lot of spilled liquid, and sometimes a pain in the stomach because you've swallowed too quickly. By stopping, you'll lose about 15 seconds but gain the full benefit of your refreshment.

When you drink, don't run.

Ten miles. Ten and 10 is 20, and then there are just 10,000 meters to go. Mind trickery? Yes, but that's what a lot of marathoning is.

More basically, experience is everything in marathoning. I constantly try to notice things that might help me in the next race, even

if they seem insignificant at the time—like some chafing that perhaps isn't bothering me right now but could in the future if I don't do something about it. Or the fact that the aid stations don't serve my favorite drink—water. Or that there's a traffic jam at the first watering hole. Or that I seem to be doing better on the uphill sections than I thought I could—a nice thing to keep in mind if there are more hills farther along.

Racing in Central Park—the 1975 New York City Marathon.

I keep track of my pacing for future reference, too. In the 1974 Peach Bowl Marathon, I set a comfortable pace, felt great halfway through, and finished in 3 hours, 6 minutes with a lot of reserve. My next long race was the 1975 Boston Marathon. Again, I set a comfortable pace and felt strong at the 15-mile point. But this time, knowing I had something left, I upped my speed just enough to finish in 2 hours, 54 minutes. If I hadn't remembered how I'd felt in the '74 race, I never would have had the courage to increase my speed, and I wouldn't have been able to break the 3-hour barrier.

You won't get to run too many marathons during your career—through 1979 I had competed in only sixteen—and you should be ready to notice things that will help you later on whenever you can.

Twenty miles.   You will go through a lot of mental changes during a marathon. You'll feel hyped up at the start and exhilarated at the

Toughing it out during the heat of the 1976 Boston Marathon.

finish, but right now you might well find yourself in a trough of depression, especially if you're running a four-loop course and have just passed the finish line for the third time. Now is the time to lean on your training. Think back over all the hard work you've put in over the past nine months. It would be a shame to negate all those fairly intensive workouts with the end so close. There are just 10,000 meters to go, and if you drop out once, it will be just that much easier to drop out the next time. Be consoled by the knowledge that most of your agony at this point is mental. If you had had a physical problem when you began, the chances are good it would have announced itself before now. Get tough.

On the other hand, perhaps you should drop out. A lot of runners boast that they've never quit a marathon. That's noble in a way, but it can also be foolish. If you do push yourself past a certain point, you'll pay for it with an injury or by having to give up a lot of running days during your postrace recovery.

A good example of this involves Ben. I mentioned that in the 1975 New York City Marathon, he dropped out—at around 16 miles—because the effort it took him to run that day was twice what it should have been. He could have finished, but for what? He would not have been able to run comfortably for several weeks. As it was, he and I flew home that night, started running again two days later, and over the next two months he had some of the best training and competitive runs he's ever had. Whether or not to drop out is a difficult question to answer. Finishing a marathon is great, but there's no point in being brought back on a shield, especially if it's a shield of stupidity. You should know your body well enough by now to make the intelligent choice.

The finish.   For the last 6 miles, you're pretty much on your own. Different people react differently to the stretch run, but if I had to guess, I'd say your first thought will be, *Let's get this thing over with.* This isn't the time for heroics. If you're struggling, try to gut it out unless your common sense tells you to pack it in. If you feel comfortable and you're maintaining a good pace, great. That's what I'd hoped would happen. Either way, when you cross the finish line and get your time card, give yourself a good pat on the back. You deserve it. Then go get a drink of something and soak your feet.

After just one marathon you will no doubt have a healthy respect for that classic distance and also, I hope, confidence in your ability to handle it. What you do next, of course, is up to you, but for now, take a couple of weeks off. Run no more than 30 minutes per day and no more than five times per week. You've just climaxed a season of running that's stretched to nine and one-half months, and you definitely need and deserve a rest. Enjoy it.

In the future, plan on running no more than two marathons per year—three at the most. Although the marathon itself should not be the most important part of your running—your daily runs are— it is probably inevitable that you will always want to lower your personal record. I do. But no matter what kind of shape you're in, it will be nearly impossible for you to run more than two marathons per year near your absolute capacity. It just takes your body too long to repair itself. Many runners enter more marathons than that, of course, but all they are really doing are some extralong long runs. If you like the competition that racing affords, enter as many races as you'd like—as long as they are at distances no greater than 18 or 20 miles.

If you take my advice and agree to run only one marathon every six months, an ideal schedule would begin with the two weeks of 30-minute runs following your marathon. Then follow the training routine outlined for Month Six of Schedule II for thirteen weeks. This will allow you to recover fully from the effects of your marathon and at the same time keep you in excellent condition.

After this period of maintenance, however, it will again be necessary to intensify your training for the next marathon. Simply return to Schedule III; only this time spend just one week on each of the nine timetables. Finally, spend two weeks cutting back your training just as you did before. Total minimum time between marathons: twenty-six weeks.

(Obviously you don't *have* to run a marathon every six months. The point is to cut back your running to the level at which you can extract the most benefit from it until you're ready to start building up again. That level, I firmly believe, is found at the end of Schedule II. Stay there as long as you'd like, and for goodness' sake don't follow my precise schedule day after day and week after week. Be flexible. Make up your own. Enjoy yourself.)

The more marathons I run, the more ambivalent I become about them. On the one hand, they are challenging; on the other, they're destructive. Too many marathoners first become obsessed by the race and then possessed by it. Maybe that's what's happened to me. I don't think so, but I don't really know either. Marathoning should not be an end, but one of many means to an end. And that end is simply running regularly, just for the health and joy of it.

12

A
Summing-Up

Sometimes it is easier to explain the worth of something by describing its antithesis.

Every so often during my daily runs I notice a woman driving a car with a bumper sticker that reads: "I'm Running. What Are You Doing for Yourself?" I cringe every time I see it. Although I've never met this woman, I've got a pretty good idea of what she's like. She is probably about my age—in her early to mid-thirties—and took up running a couple of years ago because a friend suggested that would be good for her, and besides, it was a good excuse to get away, at least for part of the day, from the everyday tensions of her personal life.

Which was fine. At first, she enjoyed her 30- or 45-minute jogs three or four times a week and looked forward to them. She lost a little weight, and friends complimented her on the fact that what weight remained seemed to be redistributing itself in a more flattering way. She started watching her diet, gave up smoking, and cut back on her drinking. She felt great and looked even better. Marvelous.

Then she got carried away. For whatever reasons, running became an obsession, and everything connected with running as well. Last year she trained for our local 10,000-meter Peachtree Road Race and became distraught when she couldn't run it because her right Achilles tendon gave way. But she's determined to enter again this year.

She keeps a daily running diary—she, of course, is a streaker and runs every day—and is disappointed when she cannot constantly lower her time. On her interval days, she carries a digital readout stopwatch, struggling constantly to knock off those 440s quickly and with regularity.

She has become a total vegetarian and would rather pass on dinner than bite into a good steak every now and again, or even a Big Mac, and ice cream, of course, is out.

She cannot talk about anything except her injuries, of which she has several because she is forever running through pain, and her training schedule. She shuns the company of nonrunners—will have nothing at all to do with them—and doesn't realize that nonrunners aren't terribly disappointed by this. Most runners wish she would leave them alone as well.

She is, in short, everything my ideal runner is not. Running rules her life, and she has the arrogance of the True Believer. Maybe you've met her.

For my ideal runner, running is not an end but rather a means to an end—in this case a life that is healthy and lived in moderation, but one that still leaves plenty of room for experimentation. My ideal runner has firm control over her life. Rather than being used by running—or being used up—she has made sure that she uses it, in whatever particular way suits her best.

In a sense, what this book is all about is experimentation. In the past fourteen years I have experimented with doctors and diets, foot plants and arm swings, training schedules and training shoes, and I've attempted to condense all of what I have learned into 220 reasonably concise pages. I still haven't hit on exactly the right combination and probably never will, but trying to find it is part of what makes living intriguing.

Although I said back in Chapter 2 that I'm not particularly fond of dos and don'ts, I realize this book contains a fair number. Whenever you encounter them again as you flip back through the pages, keep in mind that what I'm really doing is making suggestions, though admittedly some of them are more strongly worded than others. Feel free to deviate anywhere along the line and experiment on your own. It's your body and your mind, and you are the final judge of what's best. As Dr. George Sheehan says, "You are an experiment of one."

What I have learned about running, so far, is this:

•   Running is inexpensive and easy to learn, and once you acquire the habit, it will last you a lifetime.

•   Training is boring; running isn't. When running threatens to become a bore, throw away your stopwatch and your schedules, and head out through the woods.

•   There are a hundred ways to prevent running from becoming tedious. I've suggested many of them, and I hope you come up with several more on your own. Drop me a line when you do.

•   Running is so natural that running technique is relatively unimportant. If you find my section on technique and style unhelpful or confusing, skip right over it. But check yourself a few months later. You might be surprised by how closely your self-acquired style resembles what I suggested to you in the first place.

•   Run within yourself, and constantly listen to all parts of your mind and body. They'll tell you a lot. Your object is to use running as a means to total growth, and the way to do that is always to monitor your system to make sure it's in balance. Running is not an isolated activity, which is why I have included sections on stretching, weight training, diet, and even beauty care. Each in its own way can help you maintain equilibrium.

•   It is fine to be competitive, but only within yourself. What your friends and business associates do with their running is not your concern. Find your own limits, and strive to expand beyond them, but not at the expense of exceeding them. Find your teeter point, and keep just this side of it, no matter how many miles your neighbor claims she or he ran last week.

•   You will get nearly all the health benefits running affords by doing no more than what I have outlined for the last months of Schedule II—just under 4 hours of running per week, or around 27 miles. If you run more than that, you're running for other reasons. Which is fine—I do the same thing—as long as you understand that you are. Marathoning is not for everyone, but for me the running time I need to put in to help me finish one comfortably is great. It's fun to test and stretch your limits, and running marathons is one way I do it.

What's next for me? I don't really know. It would be nice to report that I am working out diligently in the hope of making the

United States Olympic team as a marathoner. But I'm not, mainly because there is no Olympic marathon for women. As the number of women distance runners has increased—several times over—during the past few years, there has been a lot of talk about adding that event to the Games, and I'm all in favor of it.

Until World War I, women were not permitted to run in the Olympics at distances greater than 100 meters. In 1928, at Amsterdam, an 800-meter run was added. A world's record was set, but unfortunately for women's running, two competitors were unable to complete the required two laps, and it was not until 1960, in Rome, that the metric half-mile was reinstated. It took another twelve years for women to gain the right to compete in the metric mile. That was our milestone at Munich; Frank Shorter won the marathon and, as I've suggested, helped touch off the running boom, for everybody.

Certainly women have proven they can stay the distance in quantity and with quality times. I did some quick figuring the other day and came up with some interesting numbers. The world's record for men in the 100-meter dash is 9.9 seconds; for women, 10.8 seconds. That's a difference of just 9 percent. At 400 meters the difference is 10 percent, at 800 meters it's 12 percent, at 1,500 meters it drops a notch to 11 percent. At 5,000 meters we women are 14.5 percent slower than the men, at 10,000 meters it's 15 percent, and at the marathon distance the figure is 19 percent.

One might make a case, then, that the greater the distance, the less equal we are, although equality is hardly the point here. But I'm convinced that the greater difference in the best man's time in the distance events compared with the best woman's is explained easily: we haven't been running that far for very long. In 1972, the first year that women were allowed to compete officially in the Boston Marathon, there were 14 entries. In 1975, my first year, the number had grown to 72. In 1978, the year I won, there were 229, and in 1979, well over 500.

Furthermore, the world record for the marathon—which is unofficial since at that distance time is determined in large measure by the difficulty of the course, and marathon courses are far from standard—hasn't changed since 1969, when an Australian by the name of Derek Clayton ran the distance in 2 hours, 8 minutes, and 3 seconds in Belgium. Since then the best woman's time has dropped from 3 hours, 7 minutes to the 2 hours, 27 minutes, and 33 seconds posted by Norway's Grete Waitz in the 1979 New York City Marathon. Waitz's time, incidentally, would have won the Olympic marathon as late as 1948.

Norway's Grete Waitz,
the women's world record holder in the marathon,
at the 1979 World Cup Races in Montreal.

The lack of an Olympic marathon for women is particularly upsetting for world-class runners, including myself, who simply don't have the leg speed to compete at 1,500 meters. If they are competitively oriented, they have no goals to shoot for. I know several women who have dropped out of competitive running in discouragement, not only metric milers who have slowed down a little, but great distance runners such as Peg Neppel, the former world-record holder at 10,000 meters.

The problems, as I understand them, are largely political. For an event to gain admittance to the Olympics, it must be contested in twenty-five countries and then gain the approval of the majority of the 160-odd voting members of the International Olympic Committee. While there are a goodly number of marathoners in the United States—more than 4,000—and Western Europe, in the rest of the world they are rare. Then there is the fact that the host city for nearly every Olympics in recent history has experienced financial difficulties. The trend in the Games is to cut back the number of events, not to add to them. The members of the IOC are notoriously slow to change, and almost all of them are men. Finally, there is a division in the ranks of those pushing for a women's Olympic marathon, especially in the United States. One group favors lobbying for a marathon right away; another suggests asking for the addition of intermediate events, beginning with the 3,000 meters, before going all-out for the marathon. In any case, the International Amateur Athletic Federation, which recommends changes to the IOC, votes only once every four years, at the time of the Olympics. By the most optimistic reckoning, it looks bleak for the first women's Olympic marathon in 1984, and not all that rosy for 1988.

Certainly the women's race would be easy to stage. Unlike other events, it could be held in conjunction with the existing men's race, with either a concurrent or a staggered start.

Although I am definitely in favor of a women's marathon, my reasons are possibly a little different from those of the majority of proponents. I am not particularly concerned about the three women who would represent the United States and each of the other countries, but I do feel that the glamour that would attach itself to such an event would do for women's running, in the United States and elsewhere, what Frank Shorter's run at Munich did for running in general—namely, attract converts by the thousands.

Probably the most important women's marathon at the moment is the International, the race started by Dr. van Aaken in 1974 and now underwritten by the Avon Company. In the absence of an Olympic marathon, it is conceivable that with sufficient sponsorship, in time the International will fill that void and become a prestigious event on its own, complete with television coverage and all the other hoopla that surrounds a major sporting occasion.

The effect, I think, would be the same either way—to get more women into their shorts and onto the streets. And for me, that is the bottom line. I am more interested in promoting running for the majority of women than I am in sending a relative handful of world-class athletes overseas every four years or even every year. But if hoopla is what it takes to get people to run, then I'm all for it.

I have somewhat similar feelings about Title IX, the federal legislation that promotes athletic equality of the sexes, in terms of opportunity and dollars spent, in the country's public schools. I think it's marvelous that the number of women's collegiate varsity

Dr. van Aaken with the American team before the Women's International Marathon at Waldniel, West Germany, in 1976.

swimming teams has doubled since 1972, that the number of basketball teams has tripled, and that the number of track and field teams has shown a fivefold increase—for those relatively few women in the programs. But if it's simply a matter of where to spend the dollars, I would rather see them spent upgrading the undergraduate intramural programs for both sexes and promoting participation in sports with a lifelong carry-over value.

Although advances have been made in the past few years, the discrimination against girls' athletic programs in high schools is still possibly the most serious example of unequal opportunity, for it's during those high school years that girls begin to form the habits of a lifetime. If there are no sports available then, it's difficult for girls to take them up on their own later. And if a high school should happen to have a girls' track program, dollars to doughnuts distance running isn't a part of it. Instead, the emphasis is probably on the sprints, where the chances of injury are the greatest and the carry-over opportunities the fewest.

Knowing what I know now, I would give anything to have had the opportunity to be a part of a track program at my high school.

I have to say honestly I'm not much of a rebel or a crusader. While I am all in favor of crusaders and their causes—most of them—it's just not in my nature to go to the barricades. Whatever influence I've had on the growth of women's running, and I hope I've had some, will have to be measured in other ways.

I've really had it sort of easy—either that, or I've been very lucky. I began running in 1966, the year that a woman by the name of Roberta Gibb Bingay became the first woman to finish the Boston Marathon (or at least the first anyone knew about). It was all quite unofficial, of course. (The next year Kathy Switzer made the news when she entered the male-only race as "K. Switzer," got a starting number, dressed in bulky clothing to hide her true sex, and officially began the race. When Jock Semple, the race director, discovered the ruse, he attempted to rip off her number. Unfortunately for Semple, Kathy's rather large boyfriend was running next to her, more or less as a bodyguard, and threw a block at him that would have looked good on "Monday Night Football." Jock went flying, and Kathy finished the race in 4 hours, 30 minutes. Unnoticed, Roberta Bingay finished again, in 3 hours, 40 minutes.)

Kathy Switzer, one of the most famous names in women's running.

Since then I have had great encouragement from my family and the support of my husband, Ben, and I have rarely encountered hostility either on the training track or in a race. I think that because I started so early—when there weren't *any* runners to speak of—I was accepted as one of the gang, without question.

I do remember one little incident, however. In 1970 I entered the Peachtree Road Race, and I won the women's division—no

great feat since I was only one of three female entrants. I got my trophy and looked at it. There was a man on top.

The next year I ran the race again, and again I won, this time beating fewer than a dozen women. No matter. The organizers were ready for me. The figure on the trophy was most definitely a woman. Things were beginning to change.

Tim Singleton hands me my trophy, with the figure of a man on top, after the first Peachtree Road Race, in 1970.

Suggestions for Further Reading

Anderson, Bob. *Stretching.* Englewood, Colo., 1975. This book has everything you need to know about stretching, and more. The author more or less published it himself, and you probably won't be able to obtain a copy unless you send $6.50, plus $.50 for postage and handling, to: STRETCHING, Inc., P.O. Box 767, Palmer Lake, Colo. 80133.

Complete Runner, The. Mountain View, Calif.: World Publications, 1974. Compiled by the editors of *Runner's World,* this volume is a collection of the best articles that have appeared in the pages of that magazine. It's also available in paperback, as are most of the other books listed here.

Cooper, Dr. Kenneth H. *Aerobics.* New York: M. Evans and Company, 1968. The first of the famous trilogy that helped popularize running for the masses. *The New Aerobics* followed in 1970, and *Aerobics for Women,* written with Cooper's wife, in 1971.

Fixx, James F. *The Complete Book of Running.* New York: Random House, 1977. The biggie, and with good reason. It's thorough, complete, and well written. As of this writing, it's not yet available in paperback because it is still on the hardcover best-seller lists.

Glover, Bob, and Shepherd, Jack. *The Runner's Handbook.* New York: The Viking Press, 1978. Over 400 pages long, this massive tome is a solid addition to any runner's library.

Liquori, Marty, and Myslenski, Skip. *On the Run.* New York: William Morrow and Company, 1979. A well-wrought account of a year in the life of one of America's best middle-distance runners.

Rohé, Fred. *The Zen of Running.* New York: Random House, 1974. A poetic collection of pictures and verse that celebrate the joys of running free.

Shapiro, Jim. *On the Road: The Marathon.* New York: Crown Publishers, 1978. A collection of portraits in words of the world's best marathoners—Bill Rodgers, Miki Gorman, et al.

Sheehan, Dr. George. *Running and Being.* New York: Simon and Schuster, 1978. Dr. Sheehan is a runner who can write and who dispenses medical advice and metaphysical wisdom with equal style and clarity. This book is mostly on the philosophy of running. For the medical side, read his *Medical Advice for Runners.*

Subotnick, Dr. Steven I. *The Running Foot Doctor.* Mountain View, Calif.: World Publications, 1977. A specialty book and a good one. If you can't find out here what ails your feet, then they don't hurt.

Ullyot, Dr. Joan. *Women's Running.* Mountain View, Calif.: World Publications, 1976. One of the first books written primarily for women, it covers a lot of territory in relatively few pages. She's said a second one is in her typewriter.

van Aaken, Dr. Ernst. *Van Aaken Method.* Mountain View, Calif.: World Publications, 1976. This is a collection by and about the man who has done so much to promote women's distance running, despite a training accident in 1972 that cost him both his legs.

Index

Aaken, Dr. Ernst van, 9, 169, 215
Abdomen stretch, 148
Achilies tendinitis, 136–37
Adrenaline, 124
Aerobics (Cooper), 31
Airola, Paavo, 172
Amateur Athletic Union (AAU), 76, 195
Anderson, Bob, 143
Angenvoorth, Manuela, 10
Ankle sprains, 138–39
Arch support, 56
Arm swing, exaggerating, 88
Ashe, Arthur, 125
Asphalt surface, 89–90
Atlanta Track Club, 7, 189
Avon Company, 215

Barbell curl, 164
Beauty care, 179–84
  for chafing, 183
  for feet, 183–84
  moisturizers, 182–83
  pH-balanced cleanser, 182
  shampoo, 183
  water and, 181–82
Be Fit! Or Be Damned!, 33
Bell, Buddy, 12
Bell, Jess, 12, 14, 26–27, 36
Bell, Julie, 36
Bench press, 162–63
Benoit, Joan, 187
Bent-over row, 163
Bieler, Dr. Henry, 172
Bingay, Roberta Gibb, 216
Black toes, 134–35
Blisters, 57, 134

Boston Athletic Association, 13
Boston Marathon, 4, 9, 11, 12–26, 29, 32, 77, 159, 187, 189, 196, 204–5, 212, 216. *See also* Marathons and marathoning
  first run, 12
  official headquarters, 12
  prerace gathering spot for, 14
  starting line, 15–16
Bowerman, Bill, 85–86
Bras, 60–61
Breathing, when running, 72–73
British Empire Games, 33
Brooks Vantage shoes, 22
Brown, Julie, 10
Bunions, 135

Caffeine, 174
Calluses, 135
Calves and Achilles tendons, stretches for, 154–57
Capillaries, 129
Carbohydrate supply, 197
Cardiovascular stress, 120
Cardiovascular system, 128
Carter, Jimmy, 31
Cement surface, 89–90
Cerutty, Percy, 89
Charles, Dr. Allan G., 124–25
Clayton, Derek, 212–13
Cloney, Will, 13
Coca, Dr. Arthur, 175
Cold weather, 63–64
Collagen, 181
Confidence, building, 40
"Cookie," in shoes, 57–58
Cooking oils, 173

Cooksey, Marty, 10
Cooper, Kenneth, 31, 33
Cramps, 139
Cushioning, in shoes, 53–54

Dalrymple, Cindy, 10
Daniel, Billy, 7
Dawson, Dr. Stan, 115, 127, 130
Dehydration, 139–40, 174
DeMoss, Penny, 24
Diet. *See* Food and diet
Diet for a Small Planet (Lappé), 176
Distance runner, image of, 32–33

Eliot Lounge, 13
Elliot, Herb, 89
Endocrine system, 118, 122, 128
Equal Rights Amendment, 40
Equipment, 51–66
   auxiliary items, 62
   bras, 60–61
   modifying according to weather, 62–
      65
   at night, 65
   shoes, 51–59
   shorts and socks, 60
   tops, 60
   warm-up suits, 61
ERG (drink), 197, 198
Estrogen, 124
Eugene (Oregon) Marathon, 9
Exercise
   preparing the body for, 116–18
   stretching, 142–58
   weight training, 158–67

Fartlek speed training, 104, 105, 136
Fawcett-Majors, Farrah, 32, 33
Flexibility
   in running shoes, 54–55
   ways to improve, 142–44
Food additives, 175
Food and diet, 168–77
   fads, 169, 170
   medical heritage and, 176–77
   nervous system and, 172
   nutritional needs, 170–71
   nutritional supplements, 176
   Stillman and van Aaken diets, 169
   vegetarian, 170, 175–76
   what to avoid, 173–74

Foot pads, 59

Gatorade, 197
George, Phyllis, 31
Gladdis, Steve, 12
Glucose, 120
Gorman, Miki, 180
Grand National circuit, 37
Grass surface, 89–90
Greece, 33
Groin stretch, 149–50
Grossberger, Lewis, 34

Hamstring, 151–53
Hard-easy theory, 97–98
Hard sand surface, 89
Heart, strengthening, 119–20
Heartbreak Hill, 21
Heat exhaustion, 140
Heel counter, 55
Henderson, Joe, 102
Hills, running on, 87–88
Hip and hip joint, 131–32
Histidine and histamine, 175
Holmer, Gösta, 104
Honolulu Marathon, 9
Hopkinton High School gymnasium, 14
Hormones, 118
Hot weather, 62–63

Indoor running tracks, 89
Injuries. *See* Pain and injuries
International Amateur Athletic Federa-
   tion, 214
International Olympic Committee, 214
Interval workouts, kinds of, 104

Jackson, Kate, 31

Kafka, Franz, 39
Kelley, John, 12

Lappé, Frances Moore, 176
Ligaments, 130
Locke-Ober (restaurant), 27
*Loneliness of the Long-Distance Run-
   ner, The* (Sillitoe), 33
Long, slow distance training (LSD), 102
Lower back stretch, 146–47

Mace, 62

Majors, Lee, 32
Marathon, plain of, 33
Marathons and marathoning, 3–8, 122, 185–208. *See also* Racing; *names of marathons*
　drinking liquids, 203
　at finish, 206
　five-mile checkpoint, 202
　fluid intake, 197
　interval workouts, 193–94
　kinds of courses, 196
　mystique about, 186
　night before the race, 198
　nine-month schedule for, 190–95
　noting landmarks, 198
　one-mile pace check, 201
　outlining a schedule, 189
　at start, 201
　at ten miles, 203
　training for, 188
　at twenty miles, 205–6
　two weeks before race schedule, 196–97
　warming up and determining pace, 199
　weekend before training, 198
Meditation, 134
Menstrual cycle, 123–24
Mental stress, relieving, 39
Merritt, Keith, 20, 22
Merritt, Kim, 18, 19–20, 21, 22, 24, 29, 187
Metabolism, 168
Military press, 161
Mind-body system, stress and, 113–26
　Atlanta study, 122–24
　how body works, 115–16
　intelligence, 113–14, 115
　responses to, 116–26
Moisturizers, 182–83
Monsport, Sarolta, 10
Morton's Foot, 137
Mount Paran Road, 6–7
Multiple-loop course, 196
Muscle, building, 46
Musculoskeletal system, 129–32
Myerson, Bess, 31

National Broadcasting Company (NBC), 12
Neck stretch, 144–45

Neppel, Peg, 214
Nervous system, 118, 128, 174
　diet and, 172
　sympathetic and parasympathetic, 132
New Aerobics, The (Cooper), 31
Newman, Paul, 31
New York City Marathon, 9, 206
Night running, 65
Non-Runners' Book, The, 34
Northside High School, 3
Nutritional supplements, 176

Obesity, 173
Olinek, Gayle, 20, 22, 24, 29
Olympic Games, 12, 186, 212, 214
Olympic marathon (1972), 31–32
Orthotics, 59
Out-and-back courses, 196
Overachievers, 44

Pace, maintaining, 88
Pagan, Thomas, 36
Page, Alan, 142
Pain and injuries, 127–40
　Achilles tendinitis, 136–37
　ankle sprains, 138–39
　black toes, 134–35
　blisters, 57, 134
　bunions, 135
　calluses, 135
　cramps, 139
　dehydration, 139–40, 174
　heat exhaustion, 140
　pulled muscles, 138
　runner's knee, 137
　sciatica, 137–38
　selecting a doctor, 133–34
　shin splints, 136
　side stitches, 139
　stress fractures, 135–36
　stress reaction and, 132–33
Partners, 95
Peach Bowl Marathon, 4–8, 77, 204
Peachtree Road Race, 32, 43, 99, 209, 217
Pedrinan, Lauri, 22
Penn State University, 70
People (magazine), 32
Peters, Jim, 33
pH-balanced skin cleanser, 182

Pheidippides, 33
Physician and Sportsmedicine, The, 123
Plante, Ray, 12
Pregnancy, 47
Preteenagers, 44–45
Pronation, 130
Pulled muscles, 138
Pulse Test (Coca), 175

Quadriceps, 153–54

Racing, 107–12. *See also* Marathons
   and marathoning; Variety and
   speed work
  diet, 108
  first mile of, 110
  halfway point in, 111
  sleeping (night before), 108–9
  splits, 110
  starting line for, 109–10
  warming up for, 109
  workouts (week before), 107–8
Relaxation, 134, 144
  importance of, 73
Road courses, measuring, 95
Robinson, Wayne, 102–3
Rodgers, Bill, 67, 159, 180
Rohé, Fred, 102
Runaholics, 44
Runner's knee, 137
Runner's World (publication), 59, 102
Running
  and beauty care, 179–84
  benefits for athletes, 46–47
  equipment, 51–66
  to improve quality of life, 46
  overdoing, 43–44
  pain and injuries, 127–40
  reasons for, 38–42
  stress and, 44, 113–26, 128, 132
  style, 67–92
  variety, speed work, and racing, 93–
    112
  workout, 141–67
Running and Being (Sheehan), 101
Running Foot Doctor, The (Subotnick),
   135

Salt, avoiding, 173–74
Schizophrenia, 173
Scholl, Dr., 59

Sciatica, 137–38
See How They Run (TV movie), 77
Semple, Jock, 13, 216
Shampoo, 183
Shea, Mary, 76
Sheehan, Dr. George, 101, 210
Shin splints, 136
Shoes, 51–59
  arch support, 56
  comfort, 52–53
  "cookie," 57–58
  cushioning, 53–54
  flexibility, 54–55
  foot pad, 59
  heel counter, 55
  kinds of, 52
  orthotics, 59
  resoling, 57
  sole, 54
  toe box, 55–56
  varus wedge, 58
Shorter, Frank, 31, 33, 168, 180, 212,
   214
Shorts, 60
Shoulders and arms stretch, 145–46
Side stitches, 139
Sillitoe, Alan, 33
Single-loop course, 196
Singleton, Tim, 15, 189
Skiing boom of 1960s, 32
Sleeping habits, 100–1
Socks, 60
Soft sand surface, 89
Sole, 54
Speed. *See* Variety and speed work
Splits, 110
Stillman, Dr. Irwin Maxwell, 169
Stopwatches, 98
Streakers, 44
Stress, 44, 113–26, 128, 132
  diseases linked to, 132–33
  mind-body system and, 113–26
Stress fractures, 135–36
Stress incontinence, 125
Stretching (Anderson), 143
Stretching exercises, 142–58
  abdomen, 148
  calves and Achilles tendons, 154–57
  fundamentals of, 143
  groin, 149–50
  hamstring, 151–53

lower back, 146–47
neck, 144–45
quadriceps, 153–54
shoulders and arms, 145–46
Stride, 70, 88, 142
Style, 67–92
 breathing when running, 72–73
 checklist for, 73–74, 77
 developing your own, 77
 foot plant, 68–69
 formal program for, 78–81
 hills and, 87–88
 hips and arms, 71–72
 lightness, 69–70
 meaning of, 76
 regularity and success, 82
 relaxation and, 73
 running flat on surfaces (first
  months), 84
 shortening stride, 70
 on different surfaces, 88–90
 Talk Test, 85–86
 and technique, 76
 time and distance, 84–85
 time schedule, 82, 83–84
 traffic interruptions, 90–91
Subotnick, Dr. Steven, 135
Summer Olympics (1980), 32
Surfaces, 88–90
Sweatband, 62
Switzer, Kathy, 216

Talk Test, 85–86, 102
Tennis, 32
Tennis shoes, 51–52
Tension, 115, 128
Testosterone, 160
Time (magazine), 34
Toe box, in shoes, 55–56
Tops, 60
Toxins, environmental, 175
Traffic interruptions, 90–91
Training shoes, 52
Tricep curl, 164–65
Truman, Harry, 39
T-shirts, 60

Ullyot, Dr. Joan, 125

University of Georgia, 38
Upright row, 162
Uterine prolapse, 124–25

Valk, Gillian, 5
Variety and speed work, 93–112. *See
 also* Racing
 program schedule (six months), 93–
  107
Varus wedge, 58
Vaughan, Ben, 127, 133
Vegetarianism, 170, 175–76, 210
Vitamin B deficiency, 173
Vitamins, 176

Waitz, Grete, 213
Walton, Bill, 128
Waltrip, Darrell, 36–37
Warm-ups, 105, 119, 199
Warm-up suits, 61
Weather conditions, modifying equip-
 ment according to, 62–65
Weaver, Eula, 36
Weight reducing, 46
Weight-training program, 158–67
 barbell curl, 164
 bench press, 162–63
 bent-over row, 163
 military press, 161
 rules to keep in mind, 165–66
 tricep curl, 164–65
 upright row, 162
Wellesley College, 20
Williams, Dr. Roger, 171
Wind conditions, 64–65
Women's International Marathon, 9–10,
 42–43, 159
Women's liberation movement, 40
Woodward, Joanne, 77
Workout (whole body), 141–67
 extracurricular activities, 167
 stretching exercises, 142–58
 weight training, 158–67

Yoga, 72, 143

Zen of Running, The (Rohé), 102
Ziegel, Vic, 34